Forever Found |  |

Forever Found

Understanding How You Belong

❦

By J.M. Crichton
as dictated by
James

First published in 2019 by J & V Crichton

Book design by Lumphanan Press
www.lumphananpress.co.uk

© J.M. Crichton 2019

Cover artwork by J.M. Crichton

The author has asserted her moral right to be identified as the author of this work. All Rights reserved. No part of this publication may be reproduced, stored in a retrieval system or transmitted, in any form or by any means without the prior consent of the author, nor be otherwise circulated in any form of binding or cover other than that which it is published and without a similar condition being imposed on the subsequent purchaser.

Printed & bound by ImprintDigital.com, UK

ISBN: 978-1-9160740-0-2

Contents

The Source • *7*

Protection • *11*

The Question of Angels • *17*

On the Nature of Angels • *22*

On Spirits • *24*

On How We Met and Started Talking • *26*

How to Talk to Your Soul Friend • *32*

The Nature of Death • *36*

Existence Between Lives • *42*

On Being Happy • *45*

About Evil • *46*

On Meditation • *48*

Astral Projection or Remote Viewing • *58*

The Question of Ghosts • *60*

On Accessing the Source • *66*

About Mystics • *68*

On the Crest of a Spiritual Wave • *70*

Hierarchy within the Source • *73*

Compatriots • *80*

Souls • *83*

On Books of Faith • *86*

The Reality of Our World • *91*

Reaching Life Goals • *94*

Auras • *97*

Energy Fields • *101*

On Limits • *105*

The Human Potential for Suffering • *108*

On Lowering Walls • *110*

On Giving Up • *113*

Compassion • *117*

Reading the Design • *120*

Finding the End of a Road • *123*

Snags in the Learning Process • *128*

The Journey from Here • *131*

Biography • *135*

The Source

THE INEXPLICABLE HAS ALWAYS BEEN a part of my life. I've always seen things that don't quite fit into the sphere of normal reckoning, and while I've sometimes struggled to understand why, I've learned to take these experiences for what they are. I've learned to accept that there is a reason for everything, and that while those reasons may not readily be obvious, they can become so in time.

Little things connect to bigger things, just as one event branches out into the world like the butterfly effect. So too do people affect one another, and concepts grow into movements so large they have the power to change the world. Perhaps my writing this book is an example of that notion in action, because now I'm here, sharing what I can with you. Now you're here too, reading this because not only do you have a purpose in reading this, you may not yet know what it is. Your goal, just as mine is, is to find that purpose and take it in its intended direction.

Perhaps you carry a message of your own, and this is where it all starts. I'm here to help you understand that. But if this is the beginning of a journey for both of us, let me start by giving you my own origin story:

Like I said, there are things in my life that I still can't explain to this very day. At four years old, I dreamed of soldiers bursting into my home to kill my family, dressed in uniforms that I would not recognize for years to come. I knew concepts of war and 'us' versus 'them' before I could fully make sense of what that signified.

As an eleven-year-old girl, I dreamed of being a man of thirty, diving into Mediterranean waters to save a child. I remember being somewhat confident but not entirely aware of whether I had been successful, but I did know that the exhaustion of fighting the waves meant I myself wasn't going to survive.

Then, when I was twelve I saw a light in my mind, a vision of a crude torch in a stone room. In this room I met a man who had not been alive for nearly 150 years, and a woman who used to make wonderful peach pies. The thing was, they were more than just a snapshot of another life. They were people with whom I could interact, and who have taught me things about how the world itself works.

The first was Jacob, the second Amelia, and while they were not the only souls to impart their wisdom and tell me their stories, there is one among them who has fallen into the role of 'teacher' with such relish that he convinced me to put together a book about it. His name is James, and this work is almost entirely directed and narrated by him.

In agreeing to dictate, my goal is to help others. Every one of us here has questions about life, death, and our purpose for being. We all want to know when we call out to something beyond ourselves whether anyone is listening, and the title of this book should always remind you of that answer. In the confusion, grief, pain, and joy of our days, we are never alone. I hope these writings serve as a source of comfort and direction, but more than anything both James and I hope you use it as a tool from which to draw your own conclusions.

Note: as you may see over the course of this book, you will see that James uses imagery more than mere words to get his points across. Sometimes his understanding of a situation comes from a multitude of angles all at once, and can take several re-reads to understand. He is not a ghost, nor is he Earth-bound in any form, but a sentient soul composed of energy. On the other hand, you may discover that he is not that different from any of us, save for his current state of being.

To that end, I'll hand over the writing here and ask for him to introduce himself to you.

> *My name, for all intents and purposes, is James. It was not the name I used in my last lifetime, which ended as far as I can tell in what was 1871 by current reckoning. It may have been the one I used directly before that lifetime, but as you will see in my writing, time is a difficult construct for me.*
>
> *I know from the chronicle of events happening in the 'physical' world that some lifetimes were earlier than others, and I can tell from my own progress as a soul where they fall into a timeline, but in my state of existence, time overlaps. I see both myself and you as everything we've ever been and are and will be or could possibly be, and that's precisely why I wanted to pass on everything that is said in this book: because the journey of the soul is something that fascinates and astounds me, even as I continue on it from a position of observation rather than fleshly participation.*
>
> *So, I hope you will allow me to end my introduction with a succinct version of why I am writing this. From the moment you come into existence until you achieve its ultimate state, you are like a diver swimming up from the bottom of the sea, seeking to break the surface and*

reach the sunlight. How you get there is up to you, and I love every aspect of that from the water to the weeds. I see the ways that people struggle and thrive and all of it leaves me in awe; it is my aim in writing this to give you the tools to learn new swimming strokes and to give you a broader perspective of the ocean around you. I hope to impart some of the joy I feel for this journey to you. –J

From here on out, all writing will be done in his voice.

Protection

I WANT TO BEGIN THIS series of musings with some basic tenets that you will see repeated throughout.

All things come from the Source, all things are an aspect of the Source, and all things return to the Source. Nothing exists outside of it, for it is existence itself. 'God,' 'the universe,' 'love,' and 'joy in its purest form' would all refer to the Source in some way. It's a concept so complicated that I could write a book strictly on its nature, but suffice it to say that it is that which encompasses everything, the pinnacle of which is a unified light/energy, a perfect happiness that knows no reason for being other than to celebrate the journey of separating from that oneness only to rediscover that ultimate bliss all over again. It exists, in simple terms, for its own sake and to understand all aspects and possible iterations of itself. I call it the Source as shorthand for something that words could never fully hope to explain.

The ultimate goal of any iteration of the Source (you and I, for example) **is** to return to it. All-encompassing joy and oneness is where we are destined for, and how we choose to get there is the whole point of why we do it. The journey is one of the most beautiful aspects of existence.

Fear is the opposite of the Source. I said that all things are encompassed within the Source, and so fear isn't separate from the

Source, but rather the idea of separation itself.

Fear is isolation; a disconnection from the Source that unifies all things. To fear is to believe there is something to lose, and if something can be lost, then there must be ownership over that thing. If ownership exists, there is already a misstep in logic, for nothing can be owned if everything is encompassed within the same sphere. There is no 'us' and 'them,' there is only 'us.' If there is nothing to lose – if we can never be separated – then there is no fear. **Hatred is not the opposite of love, but something born of fear.** Love is unity, fear is isolation, and hatred is an expression of fear. Love is and always will be both the only goal and the only truth.

Keep these concepts in mind as you read on.

I was asked whether God and the Source are the same thing, so let me say once again that they are. There is nothing in the concept of existence that is not part of the Source, and it is fine to choose your own method of visualizing what form it takes. The point of the Source is that it is all-encompassing, and that no matter where life takes you or how you change, whether you grow or fall apart, you are still a part of everything in existence. If you struggle, your struggle is one piece of an endless fabric that is forever shifting and rippling, but is at its very centre things like light, joy and endless abundance.

That is why during hard times people have turned to (and been told to turn to) the Source, to God, to help them through their problems. It is a call to remember that we are never alone because we are one with each other. The only difficulty lies in whether or not one remembers that they are technically one with that God, with the Source, rather than looking to it as a separate entity. All that would do is make a person cling to hope while simultaneously clinging to fear (isolation/separation), which dampens the effect to say the least.

The aim is to give into and merge with the Source, and I'll be showing you throughout the book how to do that.

If you hurt it is because a problem feels too big and too overwhelming for one person to handle, the best thing to do is reach out to something greater than the sum of your tiny part within the everlasting energy that exists all around you. What I want you to do if you feel like it's ever too much is make yourself bigger – and you can do that by reaching outside of yourself and drawing it all in. That means power, knowledge, peace – and all of these things can be considered to be "God."

There is no one correct way of reading God or the Source. I've said many times regarding religion that the only wrong way to approach spirituality is by encouraging fear and presuming ownership to be anything but a false construction, and I still insist this to be true. Some people say "We belong to God," and while that is one way of thinking, it's only part of the equation. "God belongs to Us" and "God is Us" are also viable and necessary aspects of explaining that relationship.

Rhetorically speaking, if the Source exists in everything, then there is nothing that we injure or love that is not contributing to something greater than just the event it goes into. Expressions of both our love and our fear have profound effects in the universe at large, and our understanding of that informs how successfully or unsuccessfully we live out our lives. That's why concepts like karma and the butterfly effect exist: because they are considering the fabric of something far larger. They are attempting to explain the scope of the Source.

I will tell you that in my last lived life I was a pretty active member of a church and even bought land to build a church on, actions towards which I have mostly positive feelings. I was part of something that sought truth, love, and higher consciousness, and I will always support that goal. On the other hand, I think it's a little bit funny in hindsight, because I remember seeing what I thought was God in things like trees and deer, smiles and kindness. I was right but had no real idea of how right I was. In all moments of life, we should say to ourselves "In this I see God" or "In this I see the Source." It can serve as both a guideline and an anchor.

There's no denomination for that concept, nor should there be if we are to remember that all things are unified. God is only a word that does a weak job encompassing a concept that is limitless. I also feel a bit of trepidation (do people still use this word?) regarding the church I helped to build, because we mixed beautiful ideas like loving one another (and thereby remembering that we are as one) with typical societal things like rules on how to behave with one another. Case in point? I was married to a cousin of mine, a soul I will refer to from time to time here as Clara, and while I wouldn't regret being joined to her in any lifetime I'm sure people would think it odd in the modern day.

The point I want to make there, and I'm sure it's a point I will make ad nauseum, is that if something has the potential to become dated, it's not something that belongs to the purest sense of the Source. It's a device of the times, a conundrum conceived simply to give people more variations on universal themes and thereby learn new ways to persevere. As I have said, the reason we are born individually and branch off from the Source in the first place is to explore every possible combination, every method in which we can return to the Source. The societies we build are merely an example of that in action.

I'm not trying to advocate marrying your cousin here! I'm saying if something is okay in some cases and not in others, you should question it. A meditation point for you to think on (of which I'm not saying there is an answer, it's just for you to consider and expound on) is this: In ancient days it was not uncommon for fourteen-year-old girls to give birth, but in the modern day it is met with disapproval. Nonetheless there is no small number of fourteen-year olds giving birth right as you are reading this, whether in a society similar to yours or one on the other side of the world.

What does that mean? What does the Source, God, think about it? Try to leave the shackles of religion and society out of your answer, and while you're at it try to put yourself into the equation as the voice of something larger than yourself. Consider points like ownership, fear, and how these life events contribute to love and joy to decide whether something is inherently positive or negative or neither. Remember that things are used to serve a purpose; whether something is a blessing or a hardship is all up to your perspective and how the world around you chooses to see it. On the other hand, remember that you are a part of that world, not a separate entity, and that your opinion counts. Your opinion counts, you are a part of the world around you and you are a part of whatever you see God as too, and with that you must strive to live up to the abundance of power afforded you whenever you choose to wield it.

I also want to go over the phrase "Go with God," because as far as the Source is concerned that is always true; you go with the Source wherever and whenever you are, because you are the Source incarnate. You may think that you are alone, or that you've changed, that you've lost your identity, that you've grown, or that you're the luckiest person on earth. In every single one of those moments, the Source is in you; it's in the air and under your feet. It's there with the person you kiss and in the fist that hits you, in your baby teeth and then your baby's eyes, in the pebble in your sandal and in the blazing bonfire. It's in the energy that surrounds every situation in your life and, much vaster than the tiny piece of time in which life you're living, it is beauty and infinity – you might experience that joy, that utter bliss, but it's when you've broken past the shell of isolation.

Bad things lock you in (think of how people curl in on themselves when they're hurt) and good things set you free (people tend to spread their arms or raise them when they're happy). We see the signs of the Source, of God, wherever we look. It's all a matter of perspective. Never feel that you are lost, only that you have misplaced your connection to greater things. Those moments are when you've lost sight of things bigger than the burdens placed upon you, and seek to rectify that situation. The Source is with you whether you remember that it is or not. The Source is you whether you acknowledge it or not.

The Question of Angels

LET'S CONTINUE WITH THE THEME of traditional spirituality and how it can help and hinder. Those I speak to often know that I am not a fan of prayers, at least in the typical sense. To me a prayer is something associated with a specific religion and as someone who has lived as part of a variety of religions, it doesn't necessarily translate. I think they tend to fit too neatly into society's boxes to be effective. Rather, what I want to say is that you don't need to direct your prayers to a specific person such as 'Grant me guidance in so-and-so's name.' No preconceived notions of God, keep your mind free of limitations in so far as you are able. All you need is the 'grant me guidance' part, and the key to it is earnestness and an open heart.

I don't want to suggest that the prayers are not heard by those with the ability to help as there is always someone watching over you, but the point is that if you insist that only one specific entity separate from yourself is able to help you, it limits your own thinking. What I mean to say is being specific in your prayers (particularly when they relate to things only true of current society) has nothing to do with the prayer and everything to do with you locking yourself into a particular construct of your society. Remember always that you are a citizen of all time and all space, that concepts are more important than their material representations. Even people's image of what God is has changed significantly over time and from person to person; we want to work in absolutes as much as possible.

Also, on this subject, it is important to phrase your prayers correctly, thinking deeply on what it is you require rather than what you want before issuing them. A person may feel very lonely and pray for a friend or for a lover, which is fine in its own way but perhaps asking for "a way not to feel lonely" or "a way to be more comfortable with your own company" may be more effective.

Be aware, too, that if you are to ask for a lover and you haven't fulfilled requirements in your life path that will allow one to enter your life, your prayer may appear not to have been granted. Rather, praying for more love in your life or to be satisfied with the love you have around you already may be the more soothing path. Love is not something that will ever be denied you; in fact, it is a matter of whether or not you are able to acknowledge and accept it as to whether you're aware of its presence in your life.

Please note that answers from outside of yourself may not always come in the form you are expecting. The problem with people saying their prayers go unanswered is that they are often looking for a specific thing to appear, when what they need to do is keep their eyes and ears open for signs all around them. Frivolous prayers tend to be answered in kind; pray for palm trees and you may receive a flyer for discounted trips to Hawaii or an inflatable palm tree at a store. Simply put, prayers never go unheard and they will always be answered in a way that follows the rules that you set out for yourself while adhering to the web of the living universe. The universe's goal is to open your mind and teach you, and even in answering your prayers it will go out of its way to point out your own hang-ups.

Still, I prefer to think of the best prayers as earnest petitions or pleas instead. Any truth you can find in this world is perfectly fine to take in a certain context, but be wary of becoming limited by that context. Open mind, open heart – always.

Now, let's discuss the concept of protection in this section as well. No one, as I have often said, will ever let you go through something that you cannot or are not meant to handle. There will be times when you as a living person, within your human limitations, will disagree with this. If you really feel that something is too much for you, you are welcome to ask for it to be removed. That sounds incredibly simple, doesn't it? Yet it's true:

If you find yourself bothered by some dark entity it's as easy as saying "Be gone!"

If you are in the throes of some emotional agony and you can't handle it any further, just ask.

You often hear from addicts and other people who have suffered horrifically that they 'offered their souls to God' in their darkest hour and they were lifted. In as far as we are all connected to the Source and are responsible for our charges, spirits such as myself are certainly able and willing to do this for you.

We cannot and will not spare people suffering in all aspects of existence because it is designed to be overcome and to enlighten, but if someone has genuinely hit their rock bottom we are aware. We're always monitoring these levels, so of course we know. If such a person asks for change, we can grant it. Indeed, in some cases we are supposed to grant it!

If you may recall various religious icons throughout the ages have been offered the same "out," but have famously refused in almost every case. There are many tales of saints and history's most respected figures choosing to persevere when they could have taken the easier, less painless route. That is the point, however: if you ask for something to be taken from you, if you ask to be spared, it's possible that you will delay your own progress and growth.

You have to consider whether or not you really do not have the strength to overcome the challenge before you offer yourself up. On the other hand, if you know without a single doubt that you have brought too much on yourself then don't be ashamed to ask for things to change. It may be a painful transition – either way it will be a painful transformation in your life, whether it is of your own strength or the universe's intervention – but you will never lose. Remember that all things are accomplished in all time and that anything you are unable to triumph over now, you will surely triumph over in another life at the very least. For smaller things, you may decide to tackle them later in the same week! Go at your own pace, as long as you aren't complacent in your own life. It's yours to shine in and no one else's.

Please also be aware that your life may take a slightly different course based on something you choose to have lifted from you. If you were supposed to overcome poverty on your own and meet the love of your life in your future financial counsellor, you may or not be able to meet that person if you receive help from a friend or some other windfall instead. If it is absolutely crucial that the two of you meet in order to fulfil one of your partner's life requirements, you may cross paths in another manner, but under certain circumstances that anticipated goal may not get fulfilled. That's why I urge you to consider seriously the gravity of the situation, but once again do not be afraid to admit temporary defeats.

The point is whether or not you have the strength within you to change the situation on your own and help yourself; if you are fighting it out of stubbornness and resistance to change, that certainly doesn't mean you are unable to fix things. If you feel in all honesty that you have been beaten down beyond that point, you merely signed up for a bit too much when you entered this life. It's a very common pattern and nothing to be ashamed of, only be prepared to see your journey head in a different direction than it might have done. You'll have to accept that.

On the Nature of Angels

I BEGAN SPEAKING ON SPIRITS and their ability to help within the scope of the Source in the last section, so let's tie that back into traditional concepts. Let's discuss what it is that people refer to as 'angels.'

The term angel is very difficult to define and is not strictly what any one culture makes them out to be. There are elements of truth to how they are commonly depicted, such as having a hierarchy, but for the most part they are just spirits in some form or another. Energy would be another way (a more accurate way, in my opinion) to refer to them. All of them were once human, just like you were once an "angel" in the cycle of existence, so to speak.

Once again, I tend to be against the traditional, society-driven depictions of things like angels. Certainly, I would count as an angel under certain definitions and we do not have wings or swords or coloured flames. Remember, that which human society has changed the image of over the centuries is limited by those depictions. It can't be a clear or accurate representation of a timeless, universal concept.

So, I suppose I'd personally define 'angels' as: spirits in non-flesh and blood form with the purpose of assisting humans or facilitating world events. Every human has at least one person watching over them to help them reach as many of their life goals as possible, and the hierarchy aspect I mentioned earlier changes with how large-scale the spirits work on. Higher level spirits work in terms of history-changing events and movements that affect ways of thinking on a fundamental level.

But as for your personally-assigned spirits? You decide your life goals before you are born and, while the beings assisting you are often people you knew in a past life (recognition makes things easier), they don't necessarily have to be.

These people are what I suppose are commonly known as guardian angels. I'd also like to point out that people often mistake guardian angels as assigned to them exclusively, which is not true. While I don't know everything about everything and there are no doubt exceptions to the rule, in my experience people are generally assigned to five or six living folk in order to guide them along. In the case that two people they have been assigned to are having crises as the exact same time, they can always call on one of the other 'angels' in order to help them out. On the other hand, it's not uncommon for the living to have several guardian angels either, particularly as loved ones pass away and insist on watching over people who were important to them in life.

I believe that we echo this sentiment in the living world as well, when we invite people to become guardians of our children or stand beside us at weddings, to take care of wills and so on. We say "I may need help at some time; will you do that for me?" and we say the same thing when we're preparing to begin a new lifetime. We say it through our prayers in times of darkness, to those who have already left their earthly vessels.

On Spirits

SETTING ASIDE THE TERM ANGEL, let's take a closer look at the spirit hierarchy. So, what is the purpose of a guardian spirit who is at the first level? To help make sure, within reason, that people reach the checkpoints they had hoped to reach before they were even born.

When preparing to come into the world, whether the first time or the hundredth of this cycle, people choose what they want to learn. They choose an overarching theme, such as humility, if they want to emotionally progress in that area. After that they choose a few points that they think will help them in that, for example: "I want to become incredibly rich and famous only to lose it all later so that I'll learn that there are more important things than fame and money." Level one spirits help nudge you in that direction, in both the good and the bad.

It's not all painful, of course; sometimes people choose peaceful lives or happy lives or lives of reflection. Sometimes they choose incredibly difficult lives that are both emotionally and physically destructive but have decided it would help them to transcend the shackles of fear, anger, jealousy or some other weak emotion. In doing so, they are also able to ask other people to help them to achieve these goals on the human side. For example, a friend who wants to learn compassion and patience may choose to be the one who gets the humility student from our example above through the ensuing fall from grace. There is an incredible amount of interconnect, as you can imagine, which requires facilitation from the other side. The most difficult thing about it, in my opinion, is watching your charge go through pain. Can you imagine watching someone in their worst hour, praying for help or respite and not being able to do anything about it because they chose to do this, because they want to be a better soul?

On How We Met and Started Talking

We met a thousand years ago – no, ten thousand years ago. In reality, we met at the beginning of time, just as we met all of our brothers and sisters. We have all known each other for always, but for some reason we were drawn to certain other souls. This attraction compelled us to break off into groups. Ours consists of just the four of us, primarily. By the four of us I mean Jacob, Clara, myself and the co-author of this work.

Names are about as inadequate as they can get to describe a soul; to me they only describe one facet of a person. They only describe a body, a single incarnation. There are others, Amelia and Lydia and Caroline, of course Caroline and her Philip from our side, but I don't know how to categorize such things. I say four because for the purposes of this writing there is the writer and me, and we come in pairs because they are parts of us too – in other words, four. It's difficult for me to discern things like telling the difference between myself and the people closest to me sometimes, which probably sounds very difficult to understand but I'll try.

So, I don't know the details of this as much as I'd like to be able to describe, but after thousands of years of soul ascension it's difficult to remember the beginning. When we came out from the ether, we were ill-formed. We barely even knew how to be people or what a person was; there were no identities. Slowly these things emerged, from which I start to believe is a sort of happy friction. Certainly, it's not our individual doing that has us becoming single identities, but I believe the universe, the Source, has a way of eking out these early beings by having them – I can't explain it well, but I want to use the word rub – rub against each other like atoms or cells. It's like we learn ourselves by learning how we are different, and we do that by forming early thoughts that bounce off of one another and eventually form a consciousness.

Think of boiling water and what you learned in science class, how water molecules will speed up and break apart – that kind of friction. Only instead of water, change it to an infinite amount of light, and within this light there are areas where this 'rubbing' is happening, and from there the souls break free of the whole. Now, as I've told you everything is the Source in different manifestations, so break free is not entirely accurate, but at the very least we can say these early souls distinguish themselves from the origin.

I guess I'm going to have to explain about soulmates now. When you start out and have those rudimentary thoughts that start to form who you intrinsically are, the person you are rubbing against is generally thought to be your soulmate. Think about it: the very reason you exist is because they exist and vice versa. Your thoughts came into being as a response to one another, so you are exactly suited to teach one another to grow and eternally grateful to one another for your actual basic existence. It's pretty incredible, if I may say so. So, to answer the unspoken question, soulmates are born at the same time. It's also possible to have more than one soulmate, though that is not what I am trying to suggest between the author and me. Maybe I am, actually, it's a bit complicated.

As you progress and grow as a soul you meet many people, all of whom share the same source as you. For some that can mean a deeper connection, one that even the living tend to be aware of via phrases like kindred spirit or "you touched my soul". If this bond continues, the edges of souls that were not born together can blur at the edges – it's like if you have let someone into your heart enough times, they become freely able to move through your energy on the outskirts. For the sake of a visual, picture a human-shaped aura or even a body, and picture a good third of the way in around the outline being suddenly semi-solid to certain other people, who when they touch that body are able to move through those pieces. With soulmates, there is no semi-solid state but rather a liquid state, and they are able to move freely within one another. I hope this doesn't sound creepy to anyone reading it, but as I have explained it is quite difficult to present thoughts that don't have a visual component in visual form. Please ask further questions for further answers.

There are a few things I want to say on the matter, being the reason why I explained this last part, and that is that even if the person you are with is not your soulmate and you know that, it is still possible to mean a great deal to one another. It is still possible to touch one another's souls and have a deep, meaningful love. I think that message is important to a lot of you out there, and I want you to know not to give up or to snub your nose at what you consider to be a lesser love. You can make a great difference to one another and in the end, we all return to the same Source, so there is nothing you can lose by loving someone as much as you are capable.

Back to the author and I, we were there together at the beginning or very close to it. We've chosen to go through lifetimes together so numerous it doesn't bear thinking about at this point and we move through one another's energy quite freely. My other half we call Clara for simplicity and hers Jacob, though I think we'll leave it at that. It can be hard to have people on the other side, for not every lifetime is suited to having both halves together.

Sometimes both halves will exist on opposite sides of the world at the same time, never meeting, which gives one the strange sense of something missing or something just beyond one's grasp. In the case that one's soulmate hasn't returned or has died prematurely there will always be a twinge of bitterness, pain and an indescribable despair that lingers in the background from one's youngest days. I'm sorry about that, but if that is what you feel like please refer to my paragraph about loving others, don't give up, and remember that the purpose you have here is to do something larger than fall madly in love (wonderful though that is). Find your purpose and make your soulmate(s) proud.

Often times the purpose is helping, as is the case here. I'm here to ensure that she is helping the people she is supposed to help by spreading the word insofar as I am able. My goal with this is to help people be comforted by the idea of eternity, not afraid of it, and to show them that they have life paths whether they feel they are on them or not. I want people to find their life paths, just as the author came back to do for some very specific people, and I figure she has the time and opportunity to help a few more. Nothing ill can come from helping people. We have been together so long and in so many ways that it's easy for me to layer myself upon her and speak through her, which is something you will have varying success with if you try it based on how close you are with the person speaking to you from our state of being. If you feel it very easily and deeply, perhaps you should start by asking where you know one another from and if the person helping you could give you some memories of one of your lifetimes together. Of course, it will be easier for you to visualize them then and therefore easier to anchor your images of your soul friend. Maybe rather than guides we'll call them soul friends.

J M and I started talking in this lifetime around the age of twelve for her. It was through her mother's meditations, through including her daughter in her own journey towards seeking a higher truth. First, she spoke to Amelia, who was close to the author in her most recent lifetime before now and made a very excellent peach pie. Jacob happens to be very fond of pies and so from there she was led to him. Realizing who he was, I think it must have come as quite a blow to her especially at that age. I think that's why I talk to her more often and more easily now. I think it's too painful to use him as a source of information for all the things she's separated from at the moment, so that's why I'm the one saying all of this. Jacob and I, as I explained earlier, have also been dear friends for as long as we have existed, so when I speak for our side I speak for him too.

The things I've said over the years have varied a lot and the way I've come across has varied a lot as well. When I first appeared to her I know she could only imagine me in one incarnation, which is I think how she would describe me now as well. I tend to appear with the colour green, often tinged with blue rather than yellow, a slightly misty or foggy undertone and I think some earthy browns thrown in here and there. That was how I first looked to her, before I had a face. After that I think I appeared in my last lifetime, which was in the eighteen hundreds and I had brown curls and green eyes. I don't think the colour of my soul, which is what she was seeing in earlier meetings, has anything to do with my eye and hair colour.

Perhaps you can see people in colours too if you meditate on it; some people find it easiest to look into complete darkness or complete light and wait for a colour to come to them so they can speak to a soul friend. I was once called James, but then again, I've been called by many names. I think James is just easier for English speakers to pronounce. Jacob, for example, is only an approximation of a much older name. Maybe you could access some memories from older lifetimes if you ask a soul friend to describe you in a different form. I feel like that is exactly the way you should ask them, the exact wording you should use: "Describe me in a different form".

I've tried to appear in a series of floating words, so that my thoughts were written out in sentence format in her mind instead of a physical self. Nowadays we tend not to use pictures of any sort unless it's something I find difficult to put into words. Similes and metaphors, for example, are easier just to display as is. I think the 'voice' as it were, my voice, comes from the back of the mind near the cerebral cortex.

How to Talk to Your Soul Friend

I ASSUME IF YOU'RE READING this book that speaking to people not currently in physical form is one of your goals. I've tried to explain at various intervals how this can be done, but I'll go into more depth here. First of all, understand that with this sort of exercise that you are not attempting to contact someone who has passed in your current lifetime like a grandmother or an old high school friend. If you start with something like that you'll drive yourself crazy because you're fuelled by grief and you also only have one image of that person to go on. Think of it as trying to contact someone in Australia based on the knowledge that 'he is called James and he has brown hair'. You don't know enough details of that person to hone in on their soul profile, so to speak.

So, we'll start with looking for someone who can help you. Go somewhere completely quiet, preferably with no one else nearby as even if they are silent their energy might interfere with your concentration. In the future when you've gotten the hang of it this won't be a problem, but for now let's just do it without interruptions. Lie down or sit in a comfortable position and close your eyes. We'll start with the more direct route first:

Imagine a wave. Not the entire ocean, just a single wave coming in and out on an unknown tide. Listen to it to the exclusion of all else, see the froth on its crest and focus on the way it moves back and forth, back and forth. Use this to clear your mind. It may take a few minutes at first, depending on how experienced you are with letting the stress of the day wash away from you. Now let the image fade to either black or white and look into that nothingness until you glimpse a colour of something. Don't try and bring it into focus, don't try and see the person there, don't do anything but acknowledge the colour and keep it central in your mind. The colour should deepen or brighten or expand in your mind's eye, but it has to do it on its own.

I think the thing that people mistake the most is that they try to chase the little progresses they make, but to chase these things is to assume you know what's on the other side. You'll inevitably get it wrong because you don't know what the manifestation will be and will interfere with its true nature as a result. Think of going into a place you've never been before blindfolded and trying to prepare yourself by imagining a hotel lobby, then opening your eyes and discovering you're in a hospital operating room. Did you do yourself any favours by presuming you were going to be in the hotel? Instead you may have tainted your own ability to react. That's why I say you shouldn't chase it.

The other major point of this exercise is trust. It sounds obvious, but people often don't realise the defences they put up around themselves. I'm not going to tell you to trust the person who comes through, all though you should. Trust yourself instead. Remember that mindfulness is the best way to keep the weirdoes mentioned earlier in this book from entering and when you are meditating and looking in yourself, that's the least likely time for anything you don't want to creep around the back stairs of your consciousness. If you find it tough to trust whoever is coming in, trust yourself to have the defences not to let that person be a bad thing. Besides, when you see that colour you are seeing a physical representation of that soul friend's personality – if you don't like it, you'll know very quickly. Hopefully you find those colours reliable or comforting, something you can feel at home alongside.

This may take several sessions, so when I describe it in a fluid motion don't feel that you are forced to accomplish things within a certain time limit. All things are accomplished in all the time in existence, if you'll recall. Once you've gotten the person's colours firmly established, it's time to make contact.

There are a few ways to do this as well, which I think depend more on the type of learner you are. Some people find it easier to process things visually, some by touch, some by sound; some are skittish and prefer to observe and some are hands-on. If you find that you prefer the visual path, ask them to show you an image. This will be easier than seeing a body-shaped version of them personally. They might show you something like a train station or a bakery, or as Jacob once showed, a sandy path winding through an ancient village. This is essentially them showing you their identification card, saying 'this is where I know you from'. You'll have to do a bit of work to process it, but from there you can start asking questions like their name and their relationship to you. I don't want you to take this at face value. I was going to say that you should, but then it occurred to me that sometimes souls don't view things the same way. They may choose a memory that to them represented glory and excitement but to you was irritating or disappointing, so definitely examine your own feelings towards the images they impress upon you. If you find audio easier to process, you might ask for a sound or the impression of a sound. If you prefer touch, move into the scene they show you and walk around. Touch whatever you like! Treat it like a dream – it is your own mind after all. They can't show you anything you can't conceive of, anyway. Limitations of the human mind and so on.

So, let's think about an alternative pathway. In your mind there is a room (I suggest this for people who are a bit anxious or have trouble giving up control) that you are going to build. What kind of room is it? Is it huge or small, new or old? What colours are the walls and are they stone or stucco, are they plastic or wood? (Authors note: plastic walls seem bizarre to me, but James insisted.) What sort of furniture is in your room? Focus on every tiny detail of this place, down to the whorls in the oak or the thread count on the sheets. Then take a seat and say, "Come and sit with me". In my opinion the person who comes to visit should be quickly apparent, though you may not be able to see them.

It's often the case that your vision will skirt around them or that you'll only see the edges, or that you won't see them clearly. This is okay, it's just an agreement between your brain and your soul friend not to traumatize you off the bat. Sometimes seeing them in all their glory will bring back a rush of memories of previous lifetimes that might be painful – and you might pine, or feel like your life was so much different then and why can't it be like that now, you might feel resentment that they're not on the same plane as you to help you through everything in a physical form. Try to remember that they are with you, though. They are.

The Nature of Death

I THINK DEPARTING CAN BE bittersweet because it's a beautiful experience but also sad. In some cases, it can be particularly sad for the person leaving, at first, because they're not used to change and they are unaware of what will happen to them 'on the other side'.

I'd like to point out first of all that there is no other side. We all share the same universe and we take our consciousness, as is, when we go. There isn't a barrier between life and death. I can't stress this enough – there is no barrier. The best way I can describe it is a child growing out of its old clothes and stepping into new ones. No one cares about the clothes they left behind, I hope, and neither does anyone think that just because the child has now grown and changed shape that they are any less the same person. Neither have they moved to some other city or country just because they're older and they don't fit into the same outfit they once did, but their outlook is certainly different and it's changing. I suppose you could say that wearing a new outfit is similar to the process of dying as well: if you've never worn fancy dress or a police uniform you'll be unsure of how to act in it at first, won't you?

People are confused and a bit uncomfortable when they cross over, usually. Think gawky teenagers getting used to their bodily changes, to continue with the metaphor of growing up. It depends on how the person died and in what capacity they left as to how quickly they get used to it, but it tends to be fairly quick. We don't work with time as such, but for the sake of perspective I'll say anywhere between one hour and one week to get used to the feeling of having returned (died), on average.

Suicides and the like often take longer. Suicides I want to say are somewhere in the three months range, comparatively. They get stuck in their own heads, stuck in their grief and guilt – they refused to accept reality to a point where they literally killed themselves, so it's understandable that they continue to refuse that in death.

I really don't like the word death, because it's ...misguided. It precludes all the changes and transitions that occur, I think. Death sounds like stopping, but there is nothing 'stopping' about the process whatsoever.

So, back to suicides, which is perhaps a strange place to start: they tend to relive their pain over and over in a PTSD sort of way. A lot of it is regret, I think. They absolutely do not want to see the people they left behind, at first, because even to us who have settled here the thought of causing pain is reprehensible. They feel as though they've failed, that they've done horrible things to hurt the people they love and they feel, as I say, incredibly guilty. But they're only looking at one part of the big picture, one tiny iota of reality. We can try and pull them back from it, but it's a long and difficult process and tends to be one they have to go through themselves. Afterwards, these types usually watch over their loved ones from a safe distance. They appear from time to time but don't spend every waking moment with them because they want to give their precious people a chance to move on and continue with their lives. Also, because it's painful to watch people go on without you when you finally realize that you were meant to be a part of that life, as opposed to other methods of dying. I want to get something straight here, no matter how harsh it may sound: suicide is a failure.

You are never born with the purpose of killing yourself (throwing yourself in front of a car to save someone doesn't count). You are never born with the idea that you can't handle what life is throwing at you. It can be awful, and it can really be more than you thought you'd be able to handle when you planned out the learning process, but it's never meant to be anything other than a challenge to which you should rise. At times we'll try and set things straight by making the bullet miss or the rope fail, but in some cases, it's going to happen. Particularly if it's very obvious that a young soul signed on for way more than they were ready to handle.

The other thing I'd like to say about it is that a failure is not as bad as the word makes it seem. Remember the saying 'you haven't failed until you've stopped trying'? For the concept of eternity to ring true, there is no such thing as to stop trying, so there's no possibility of actual, permanent failure. And no one here is going to hold it against someone for not succeeding at a life; we've all been there and besides, even things like that can teach us about ourselves. The next time we'll just have a better idea of what we can withstand.

So, we move on from self-induced death to violent death en masse, as I think I covered the reasons people might agree to be killed on an individual basis in the previous entry. This takes a lot of coordination and cooperation on our side, which sounds awful I'm sure. Let's take a situation where sixteen people are supposed to die in a shooting or a crash of some sort. That requires sixteen people, before they're born, to agree to go in this manner at this time. That means that they have to be able to accomplish whatever goal they wanted to accomplish before they pass away, whether that's at sixty years old or six. Often the goals of these people, when they're born, are largely for the sake of other people around them. There's a reason that when you hear these people talked about on the news they're described as angelic, as wonderful and kind and inspiring types. That was their reason for being and their reason for dying too. The trauma of such an event inspires the people caught in the ripple effect of it to change their lives, whether by virtue of running out of time to complete their own goals or living the portion of life they felt was lost by that person who passed away in their prime.

How is this all accomplished? Well, the helpers (angels?) of the individual people who are going to pass have to be informed and ready so that they can receive their charges at the moment of death. In some cases, there will be survivors, so the person's watcher will need to protect them in what is often referred to as a miracle; this can be quite difficult and require the cooperation of people higher than them as well. The people above that who are coordinating on a localized level (immediately surrounding the events) need to make sure that things go smoothly, that nothing outside of the scenario is caught up in it and that the people who are responsible on the living side for causing it are monitored closely. The impact on the world and people not directly tied to the situation is taken care of by the level directly above me and if it's a massive event the level above them, but they deal more in abstracts. The world will realize it's time to stop the racism and new bills will be enacted, that sort of thing.

I hope that covers the topic of mass transitions.

For people who are caught up in a long-term illness, it tends to be a case of something they challenged themselves to as a way to find clarity. Suffering brings enlightenment, sadly. We think of darkness versus light, that they both need to exist in order to highlight one another, so a lot of great wisdom comes from suffering. History can tell you this; just read about a war survivor or a cancer survivor and you'll know. The positive thing about passing away after a long illness is that a great deal of older souls will have long been ready to go and the moment they transition is just so easy. They tend to say, "What took you so long? I've been waiting for ages!" and there is no thought of pain. Pain ceases to have meaning well before they actually die, once they've put it together that that's what's going to happen. We tend to collect before the actual throes as well, if that's any comfort to you. I'm sure you know it as well, in your heart, if you've ever had the mixed blessing of witnessing someone pass before.

Let's think about kids for a second. How awful is it that tiny babies and other people who haven't yet begun to live have to die? How heartbreaking? I agree, it's very tragic. I can vaguely remember crying like a madman when some of my babies passed away in infancy in other lives, though I'm ashamed to say it feels distant now. Well, not ashamed for the sake of myself because I know what it's all about, but ashamed because I would like to maintain compassion for those in pain, as is often the case with the living. Still, the point of these little ones is the impression they leave on the lives of those who remain. They are very often souls who don't even need to return, who agreed to come back just for the sake of creating a meditation point for those lucky enough to be with them for that short time. They tend to have one of two characteristics: they seemed to know more than they should have; they were wise beyond their years – or else they were as innocent and pure as the driven snow, fueled by pure love. The lives they touch are irrevocably pushed in a direction of enlightenment and a search for meaning, or perhaps the people left behind find a purpose in helping others or helping themselves. That's the entire reason those children are ever born. Don't mourn their loss, be thankful for their visit.

Finally, let's talk about passing away peacefully in one's sleep as everyone aspires to it. My my, if this happens to you, you got lucky! It also suggests you've lived a very good life and didn't have anything left to accomplish. No one passes away from natural causes, unconscious, without having completed everything on their task list. It's like the gold star of life times. Also, you don't get to choose this ending funnily enough. No, you can choose to go any other way you'd like but you won't get to know how you pass until you're on the other side if you pass that way. You don't say goodbye, you don't plead for your life, because you don't need to anymore. You're fine with it and the people you left behind will hurt but they will also understand. If it doesn't happen for you like that, don't be too disappointed though. You really need to have achieved a high level of peace for that to occur and sometimes it just doesn't work out that way.

Existence Between Lives

I THINK OF THE IMAGE of being 'in between' lives as being centred on the body-based state, which is only one tiny aspect of existence. I've said it before and will say it many times henceforth, but there is a reason the word universe contains the concept of oneness. All of you is you; though it sounds extremely simple it is a difficult concept to wrap your head around. Whether you have a beating heart or just the memory of one, you do not cease to exist in an infinite state. If you were once a fifty-year-old man and now you are a thirty-year-old woman, you must be something that is simultaneously both of those and neither of those people, correct? Think of waking and sleeping – are you suddenly a completely different person or being just because you're in a different state of consciousness? Not at all, but you may glimpse a bit of the difference if you view it from the dream world.

When you dream, do you find that you are able to move faster or that things around you move at a different speed? Can you know things and do things that you wouldn't otherwise be able to in the waking world? That's remarkably similar to how things are when you aren't limited by a physical form. You can manifest thoughts into images and manipulate the situation at will, if these things are generated by you. Alternately, if you are invited into – a manifested scenario, shall we say – you will have some ability to control the situation. This is how we tend to appear in dreams, too.

Have you ever had a dream where someone you lost appeared and they seemed to tell you things? Perhaps they were able to produce a flower and hand it to you or conjure some symbolic imagery? That's because they were invited in, whether by your desire to see them or the fact that your heart was open to them. Rest assured that if they were intending to harm you (and such people – things – exist) they would not be allowed in. Not only do you have your own defences to prevent that but those who watch over also function as guards to your consciousness. So, what happens when you don't remember your dreams? Do you simply cease to exist? Of course not!

The reason I say this is because you don't need physical imagery to have thoughts. When you are in physical form, the easiest way to process an idea is by giving it a corporeal aspect even in your thoughts. We say 'picture this' because the biggest difference between being in the flesh and not is sensory. If you could no longer see or touch or smell or experience the idea of a table in any other way, would you be able to describe a table? I suppose you would describe the memory of a table from this lifetime. Now try thinking of a table from one of your other lifetimes, or if you're not able to picture a table that you have heard existed in the past. Now think about the multitude of shapes and sizes and materials that tables have ever existed in and tell me which one of these things is a table. Now tell me how important the image of a table is versus the concept of one. There you go.

When you're sleeping and not officially dreaming, that's what's happening. Your consciousness is still running but it's not close enough to the surface world to require translating it into images.

On our side, this also happens. We on our side are pure energy essentially, but it doesn't mean there aren't thoughts happening still. When we speak to the people who are in human vessels, we may speak with varying degrees of eloquence using physical representations of functional concepts. That's why it's sometimes clumsy or incomplete, so forgive us for that. Still, the next time you are trying to connect with someone in a similar position such as myself, remember that there is that lost in translation problem to contend with.

As you start out you will probably get a jumble of images that flicker in and out, then perhaps you will learn to anchor to those images – recall that it is you needing to anchor to those pictures and not the one on the other side. Eventually you may be able to move beyond images and into directly projected sensations that are much more fluid and quick to speak with. And finally, remember that one day you will not have need of the physical whether it be your body or your possessions. Memories are all about how they made you feel, not the sensations. You can take those sensations with you.

It is for all of these reasons that I say you may be a fifty-year-old man and yet a thirty-year-old woman. You are all of these things in the concept of the individual soul that partakes in the process of ascension over many lifetimes and many tiny enlightenments. Remember too, in the idea of the universe – you have been all of the people you see, somehow and somewhere. They are all you because we are all you, you are all us, and we are all one thing in the end: pure joy, which manifests in love.

On Being Happy

GREAT PEOPLE ARE SYMPTOMS OF a movement, not vice versa. Even if they are born to be great leaders, the Happiness is a side effect of self-realization. Doing what you were meant to do brings a sense of satisfaction and belonging, while straying from the path you've set for yourself brings pain and depression. Everything from vices and addictions to ruts and stagnation are symptoms of straying from your purpose and will distract you from what you were meant to do. Existential pain happens because you have an internal compass, functioning so as to point you in the right direction. Whenever you feel empty, in particular – that's when it's time to face the truth. It's not working for you because that's not what you're meant to do. To be happy, you must self-realize, and to self-realize, you have to first discover and then dedicate yourself to the life you were meant to live.

About Evil

I'M GOING TO TALK TO you briefly about the concept of evil, which is a pretty heavy topic and one that people often ask about. Shall we start with polarities? If the Source is joy and love and wholeness, evil is fear and fracture. We could break evil down into an immeasurable number of categories, but at its heart it would always be fear. And in particular it is fear of loss and fear that there is no continuation after life. So again, fear: fear stems from loss, fear stems from the idea that there is no such thing as infinity and that there is no such thing as an everlasting abundance. Fear is to be separated from the whole, which is only ever self-imposed. There is no way to exist outside of all of the things that have ever existed, is there? So why would you ever imagine that you were alone? You're not thinking big enough, not seeing the grand picture.

Still, in mortal brains this fear arises because people don't remember the everything that they have been and they certainly don't remember that what they do to each other is essentially what they are doing to themselves. Jesus had it spot on when he talked about the least of his brothers. What I think he also might have been trying to say is 'that you do unto yourselves' as well. I'm also a big fan of "any man's death diminishes me", to quote John Donne, because subconsciously the public feels the loss of people they don't know and there's a reason for that.

I know it sounds strange but people kill because of fear of their own mortality. By kill I don't only mean murder, but everything from rape to putting another person down.

When people are awful to each other it's because they assume that they have the ability to own and that means that things can be taken from them. Rather than own, I want you to say 'experience'. You experience the scenarios a video game provides you with, but the idea of owning it is a construct. Do you own the plastic? Do you own the idea that someone else came up with? Does the person who came up with the idea also own the work that went into it by the graphic designers and programmers? How about the people who manufactured it and marketed it? How much do they own and how much do you own? There is no such thing as ownership, **only** experience.

Covetousness is at the centre of what we call evil for two reasons, because it assumes that we can own and therefore that we can lose. From there springs the fear I mentioned and from that evil acts. You can't take it with you, but as I said in the previous entry you can take with you how something or someone made you feel, therefore in your own life try not to covet and try not to fear.

There are bigger, more important things than that. The sooner you move away from these things, the sooner you will be able to find the joy and the abundance you seek. Don't trap yourself in isolation, because trying to isolate yourself will only lead to pain and worry. It's against the natural order of things.

On Meditation

I RECOMMEND MEDITATION OR SOME other spiritual endeavour. If you want to go to a church or other place of worship, be my guest – just remember that the entire purpose of any soul-searching activity is to see beyond the present and the tiny chunk of universe you're currently residing in. Then try and be fine with it in all of its vastness, and see it as neither here nor there, and look for joy in its purest form, as it exists in everything. Tough, right? But you might get there nonetheless!

* * *

This section gets into my personal experience with meditation over the course of various lifetimes. I suppose it could be put down to the path I chose to get where I am today and as you may have gotten from my voice thus far, it's not something I usually talk about. We think that when we reach the end of our lives that all the pain and betrayal, all the hardships we went through, will be with us – but they won't. No one wants to lay on their deathbed thinking of the time that their mother didn't show up for their school play (I wasn't ever alive for such events, incidentally) or the time that they went hungry and cold. They think of those moments of happiness, no matter how few and far between they may have been. That should be your first hint at the key to enlightenment or else progress in general.

I'd also like that to serve as a disclaimer, because for me the parts of my lifetimes that I tend to remember are all the great ones. I remember the colour of my beloved's eyes and the feeling of being hopelessly in love, of seeing great sunrises that brought tears to my eyes. I think of watching my children grow in safety and contentment and I think of moments where I witnessed history, where I knew humanity was standing at the precipice of yet another monumental leap. I don't even think of those days when I was alive at the end of a battlefield, happy to be alive as I was, because it was so ill-wrought. I don't consider overcoming hardships to be the goal so much as I consider hardships themselves to be a matter of perspective. Hamlet really had it down pat when he said, "O God, I could be bounded in a nutshell, and count myself a king of infinite space—were it not that I have bad dreams."

Well then. How did meditation affect my living life? I think that throughout various centuries, whether my skin was browned in the sun or pale from years of freezing rain, regardless of my religion, meditation helped me to connect to the Source and get out of the tiny space of my own skull. I always, always loved the idea that I was bigger than myself, that I could connect with something so massive and all-encompassing as music or even the great endlessness of the sky. When I meditated (and here I call prayer a form of meditation) I opened myself up to bigger things and I tried to create a tether between myself and the infinity that I call the Source.

One major difference was how I pictured it. Sometimes I saw human-like figures, sometimes animals, sometimes winged beings and sometimes all I saw was light. My image of what I saw was painted by the world I lived in. I'd like you to try picturing this as well; if you have a particular deity in mind, you can use their face. If you don't, imagine the person that you admire the most in the entire world, whether it is a historical figure or someone you knew that has passed away. Picture them backlit by white or yellow light that slowly surrounds them and they fade into it, become one with it. In this way you are seeing your own ideal and how it relates to the Source. Remember, all things come from the Source and all things return to it. Whatever form they currently hold is only one facet of something too great for us to comprehend, so of course it's okay to use some sort of imagery to guide us there.

That is all prayer is and therefore all that a particular religion should be comprised of: a way to access all the things that we are capable of, not just that we are commanded to do but that we are inherently capable of, translated into a shape that human minds can comprehend. And that's what we're all aiming for, isn't it? That ideal form of self that we want to achieve in order to let go of that evil, that wrong sense of possession that separates us from others and locks us in our own mind. We want to let go of our fear and connect with possibility without limits.

And so, in my own lifetimes I often found myself asking for strength and to be a better person. I'm not sure that that's how it worked, now that I look at it from this side. How can you ask for a strength that you don't already have? Alright, against my better judgment I will provide you with a particular anecdote from a country that doesn't exist anymore. The blood of those people still runs through those living in the modern day but their particular tribe (at the time my tribe) doesn't exist anymore.

It was a rocky, cold place that I believe is somewhere near Romania these days. We were more closely related to Greeks, whatever that means to you. It was freezing cold and it rained constantly during one wintery season; we had no food and we lost two of our children then. The days felt as dark as I felt on the inside, and now that I think back on it I don't think I was able to cry half as much as I wanted to at the time. I remember our tiny baby going blue and I remember tears on the day she was buried and after that all I can recall is this unending emptiness, this numbness because I didn't have space, I felt, to mourn her after we'd lost a seven-year-old girl as well. I was so deep in despair. My biggest problem as I see it now is that I had lost the ability to connect with others and I was stuck in my own head. I know now that the lesson I was supposed to learn that lifetime was that going through the motions is not enough and that it means you haven't reached out to everything that is around you. I remember an elderly relative who I think may have been my mother (people aged very differently in those days) telling me that the world was all around me if I chose to be a part of it. I had no idea what she meant at that time, but I also remember feeling the exact opposite as well. I remember having the icon on my wall that I could have used as a guide to open my own heart and thereby relieve some of my own burden but I saw nothing more in it than a twisted piece of wood.

I can recall seeing the mountains that surrounded the place we lived, a place I think would be too small to call a village, and thinking they were locking me in instead of what I could have thought which was that they were an extension of me. The mountains were part of my life and they had formed me in that lifetime, just as that hard ground that wouldn't give us a damn root vegetable to live off us was. If I had seen just a little while into the future I would have seen my remaining children grow up and for the meagre crops to return. I would have seen my mother for how wise she was, would have appreciated the infinitely forgiving Clara by my side and I would have seen that my kids were pretty amazing people. They grew up to be people that even now I can say I'm proud of, but at the time I was an idiot. The best I can say is that at least I wasn't cruel, and if that's the best you can say about a lifetime you're just going through your paces and no better. Learn from my mistakes there. Connect with things bigger than you.

I think the underlying point I want to make with all of this is that you can carry as much as you give yourself the capacity for. By contrast I want to use someone else's life centuries away from that – perhaps much as a thousand years apart now that I think of it. This is not a story about myself so much as I was an observer who lived a pretty mediocre if happy life in that scenario. In a thousand lifetimes I've attended religious ceremonies and services, but in this particular lifetime it was the local priest himself who taught me things that I would like to contrast with my previous story.

This man was married after he moved very young into a village of pretty dramatic goings-on. A local lord disowned his son and was later accused of pushing him down a staircase to his death, while another man had crippled his wife from beating her, a young boy fell off a horse and died and I'm fairly sure at least one of the priest's own children died from a fever.

The common cold was quite deadly in those days. The weather, in my opinion, was even worse. The people of this village would come in to his church every week and expect the moon from that man, and every week he would absolutely deliver. He gave the most moving speeches about our capacity to love and to forgive, and I recalled him always saying that we should be given room to be the greatness we were meant to be. It wasn't that he clung to that belief either, it was settled in him like stone. He never looked at people as deformed or unnatural and he didn't even refer to people as alive or dead. He always spoke of them in this strange present tense that I now know meant he was referring to them in their infinite form but at the time just sounded completely magical to me. To the townspeople too, particularly after the wife-beating man passed away and his widow immediately took up with the kindly gardener who had pushed her around in a cart for years just out of the goodness of his heart. The priest told us that the man had failed to see the goodness in himself and make the best use of it and that he hoped the man would do better in future. It was extremely unorthodox I believe, but it has always stuck with me as something I should have known in earlier lifetimes.

Incidentally, that man is not a Level 2 or 3 or 4, but still remains at level 1. I want to impress that upon you just because it is possible to absolutely master some of the lessons you are meant to learn well before you reach this 'perfect' phase of understanding that allows you to move up. It doesn't all come together at once and certainly not in the same order for everyone, but when that last piece of the puzzle comes it will form a complete picture. And again, the keys to meditation no matter what your outlook on life is are one, to find a point of focus that represents everlasting joy, love or peace and two, to use it to expand the space within yourself. Bringing yourself beyond the confines of your shell and extending your inner capacity are the goals to finding all of the answers to these secrets of life, and that shell may refer to the body you are currently located in, to your outlook on life or even to the situation you find yourself in. Perspective, as I say, is everything. Try not to centralize it so much.

Meditation can only get you so far. By this I mean meditation removes you from the hustle and bustle of daily life and it can serve as a reboot or a refresher, but once you are back in the situations that caused you to build up stress in the first place it can be hard to maintain a level of serenity that would allow you to better deal with those situations. What I want you to know is that meditation should serve as an anchor instead of an escape; it should be something that trains you to access a place of calm and comfort at any point in your life, whether you are awake or asleep. Yes, meditation is a key point for someone who is suffering from recurrent nightmares! It's the first thing I would ever suggest if someone told me they had bad dreams every night.

The reason for this is that dreams are a product of things we are unable to resolve in our waking lives, whether the situation is unaddressable or whether we refuse to face them. The point of dreams is to work through fears, solve problems and acknowledge hidden anxieties. I'm not going to go into something so complicated as a dream dictionary, but the easiest way to determine why a dream has happened to you is to ask yourself: How did I feel? How would I describe key points in the dream? Were they menacing or comforting? Did that person feel like an authority figure, were they on my side? Once you've answered that, you should apply it to a current (or still emotionally relevant) scene in your life and layer it on top – the answers should come easily.

But say you want to get some rest and avoid rehashing everything that is bothering you in your life – the answer to that is meditation before sleeping. It's not enough to lie down and use the time you'd otherwise be reading to rest your mind; you need to make specific time, a minimum of twenty minutes, of meditation for meditation's sake prior to going to bed in order to resolve your emotional turmoil. If the anxiety or the dreams are very bad, I would suggest upwards of an hour. Anything longer than that is, quite frankly, escapism.

I feel like that statement may be polarizing for some, but as I said at the beginning of this section the point of meditation is to function within the world, not remove yourself from it. If you choose to spend hours and hours of each day meditating (particularly if these hours are consecutive) you are only spending less time in the world you live in. If you meditate properly and reach goals within those meditations, the effects of clearing your mind will stay with you and you will be able to use the tools you've learned without stepping away from the world in order to do it.

The aim that all meditation should have is to answer questions and teach you how to access your higher self. It's good to spend as long as you need calming yourself first and emptying your mind, whether it's by picturing solid black, solid white, grey clouds or smoke, picturing snow or the movement of waves. The point of what you need to imagine is that it expands beyond the edges of your vision; it is something able to continue on into infinity, beyond what the eye can see. People are told to focus on their breathing, but the reason that is said is to establish a slow and steady rhythm so the sound of wind moving back and forth, waves crashing, even a low, even drum beat could work if you find one clicks better with you than another. So: step one is use as much time as you need to picture an infinite, steady picture and set an even, steady pace in your mind.

From here you have several options depending on what you need to do.

If you are suffering from anxiety, the absolute last thing you should do is address the problems individually. **Do not** bring them back up or you'll lose everything you just cleared! The point here is that you are able to solve your problems, all of them – you are capable of anything as long as you are of a mind to do so.

Picture a golden light filling you and filling the room, the house, the neighbourhood, the city. Reach it all the way up into the cosmos and say 'I am huge of soul, I am infinite, I have no boundaries. Nothing is beyond me.' Or you can picture your own soul, a thing of energy occupying your body in whatever colour you choose, and imagine pushing it beyond the barriers of your mortal flesh, reaching out as far as you can manage. Tell yourself, "I can manage whatever I need to; I have access to as much help as I want or need." Just keep repeating that until it is solidified in your brain, until it is something that you have accepted as creed or mantra in your bones.

With repetition, it should be easier to access this expansive sense of self in your waking life. Every time you feel alone, overwhelmed or want to cry all you need to do is take a breath and fill that breath with the knowledge that nothing is too much for you. As you push that breath out, so too push your energy out and broaden your soul to accommodate the size of the situation.

If you are in pain, on the other hand, it is best to imagine something that is physically soothing. You can imagine cool water surrounding you, soft flower petals brushing over you, healing hands kneading your sore muscles or running your hands over a soft animal. It may seem counterintuitive to picture a physical thing while meditating away pain, but physical pain has a physical source; you need to redirect the signals your body is telling your brain. I would recommend no mantra or chant in this case because language is mental and will only get in the way of telling the rest of your body that it is doing something else. You are reprogramming your nerves with an imagined situation, which in time will grow more real and be more accessible in your daily life. If, for example, you were struck with severe pain in the middle of a supermarket you may wish to imagine a peaceful forest layered over the cans and vegetables all around you, or maybe that you are wading through a tranquil pool even as you make your way through the aisles. Whatever meditation does for you, it needs to have an anchor so that you don't need to wait for your inner peace. Sometimes having to wait can be the difference between life and death.

Finally, if you are hoping to access answers from the so-called 'other side.' (I feel 'other side' is a misnomer; I would say they are layered upon one another or next to each other but certainly not separate!) In that case you begin by clearing your mind completely and you open yourself, unfurling your mind like the petals of a flower or like closed hands relaxing. You wait, you invite. You don't search. I suppose for the purposes of this meditation please think of searching for them as trying to coax a small animal onto your hand. Certainly, we aren't such timid creatures, but the nervousness that accompanies reaching out for contact can ruin the platform for us to arrive. Don't expect anything, don't try to imagine what they are like, just remain calm and open and accepting. You should have an appropriate amount of protection both within yourself and from those who watch over you to allow it to happen without fear of letting something negative in. The point is you don't have to do anything, you have to be willing to let it happen. For many people that is the most difficult part; but after the first few times you manage it, it will grow easier and easier and you will have access any time you like. That in itself is comforting, isn't it?

What I would like to say, above and beyond anything else here, is that meditation is not an escape. It is a way to be in tune with that you that has existed and will exist forever, to act as a sort of self-healing and self-teaching. You should never consider your meditation time as separate from the rest of your life, not in your conscious life. What you get out of meditation is available to you whenever you want it, as long as you know how to reach for it.

Astral Projection or Remote Viewing

WHY WOULD SOMEONE WANT TO astral project? Two reasons I can think of: first, for an expanded perspective on your life and the universe, and second, to realign your energy with the world around you and the energy that exists in all things. So, as you will read in other sections of this book, fear is more or less equal to isolation, which is the opposite of connecting with and merging with the Source and with energies beyond yourself. Therefore, the first step to achieving an "out of body experience" is to get rid of any fears you have.

Are you scared of encountering a demon? Scared of the (irrational) possibility of being unable to get back in your body? Get rid of them. Learn to overcome them. Nothing will hurt you on the other side and the "silver cord" between you and your body can't be broken.

Do it after you wake up in the morning: Set your alarm clock an hour early so you feel a bit drowsy. Relax your body: Let the tension out, get rid of any random thoughts. Relax.

Imagine: Focus on a specific part of your body (your toes) and imagine that it's moving (curling your toes) but don't physically do it. Spread that out slowly to the rest of your body.

Imagine again: Imagine yourself getting up and moving around your room while you're still lying down.

Vibrations: You should feel vibrations. It's trying to channel you into the astral plane.

Practice: The above steps take a lot of practice and patience. Once you've managed to do it. Have fun and be safe. Explore the world and even outer space. Getting back into your body: The silver cord will always guide you back.

Side note: Try and 'present' or strengthen your aura when petitioning the universe. First, you're saying 'me! It's me who needs it!' and second, you're reaching out and tapping into the infinite – James

The Question of Ghosts

SOMETIMES FEAR GETS US... STUCK. If you get stuck, you aren't seeing the big picture and sometimes this happens to people as they die. They can't let go of the past and the present pain, maybe even guilt, and as a result they might linger on the human plane in the space in between worlds, clinging to a human form even though it's not necessary. If you've ever seen those paranormal photographs of the so-called angels we talked about before, you know that they appear as a shapeless form of light, right? Why can't we see their human shapes? Because they don't need them! Now think of what a picture of a ghost looks like – vaguely human, right? And not as bright. It's because they're unable to tap into the whole, into the infinite energy that I have tried to describe to you in this book.

Again, imagery is not necessary to those who work from straight thoughts and sensations rather than the slower, more human form of needing pictures. Ghosts appear in somewhat human form not for you, to scare you, but for themselves. They're afraid of losing the form they took in living life.

Now, people may also think that ghosts in a haunted house are 'after them'. That doesn't make much sense if you recall that they aren't seeing the big picture and that's why they're stuck. Generally speaking they are trapped in their own fear loops, replaying what-ifs and bad memories over and over again to the point that they aren't even aware of anyone else around them. If they are, because of the self-imposed pain and fear that they are reliving, they are more likely terrified of anyone who wants to reach out to them.

Sometimes it's nearly impossible to make sense of what a ghost is saying because it's just incoherent suffering and in some cases anger. Think of your movies and how people deal with trauma – what happens when someone tries to approach them? Either they collapse in a sniffling ball or they lash out, sometimes running away. Ghosts are far closer to living humans than those on my side.

Sometimes the things you might see in a haunted house are not actually ghosts either, but imprints of energy from strongly-felt events. I wouldn't say that all imprints are negative, but people tend to notice them more when they are. I would say these things are like a memory loop, replaying tiny pieces of history over and over again. The energy extends through everything though, and as a result people pick up on them. They are manipulated by the negative tone the energy in that spot has taken on. Some people who have tapped into the Source a little better may be able to right the energy in that place, if they can see it.

If you're looking for a fun project you can practice trying to see the energy of a place as well. I recommend looking at it as if it is a grid work, just for the imagery that the living so require. Any healing work you can do on a site is absolutely worth it, no matter what form it takes.

So, things that aren't ghosts. Things that your consciousness requires you to be protected from. Remember how I said that it takes most people the equivalent of a week to settle after they pass or maybe up to three months for suicides and other heavily traumatized persons upon crossing over? Sometimes that doesn't happen, some just don't go through the transition. It's an incredibly rare case and awful, awful, awful to talk about. I feel sick thinking of it, in so far as I am able to feel these things. Regret, I suppose, is the best way to describe it, but I am a small fry in the universe still. If I think of the Source, I recall that there is no beginning and no end. These people are not lost, but they are returned forcibly to the light. That is to say, they have to start again.

It's not like we just decide to pull the plug on these people, please don't think of it like that. They are given every chance to find their way back and their loved ones as well as people who have always watched over them try and show them the way. They isolate themselves, they are stuck in fear and the narrowest possible image of the world. They are, in their own minds, cut off from all the things that connect us to one another and they are cut off from the pure joy that exists. That makes them incredibly dark.

Remember when I said this sort of thing is incredibly rare? Think of one blade of grass in a several acre field. It is **not** something you need to worry about or fear that has happened to anyone you have lost. I'm only trying to explain the concept of ghosts and not-ghosts as pertains to evil and as to how they can be allowed to exist in the first place. Well, what you may call demons is what these things become. They certainly are not stronger than I am in the opposite direction, though they may choose to manifest in actual darkness or appear in visions if they get out of hand enough.

Remember, they have lost their humanity in one sense, because they have tied their existence to one tiny aspect of themselves, and refuse to see anything larger. The difference between them and ghosts is that they crossed over first, essentially. Once again, we give them every opportunity to pull out of it if they can and do our utmost to help them. Sometimes it doesn't work and they have to be …I don't want to say destroyed, but separated from their individuality perhaps. They are sent back to the Source, to everything, at which point I'm not sure of the details beyond that they will be able to be reborn as a soul once again. I don't know how long it takes, because I'm fairly sure at that level there is no such thing as how long. Its magnitude is even beyond what I can comprehend, but rest assured that they do come back. I have seen souls being born before; I know the way that one can intrinsically know something that this is the case.

One more thing – two more things – which I hope are relevant to this subject. Don't suppose that these things that go dark are necessarily mass murders or the people who were most evil in life. I'm not sure that I've ever seen that happen before. Usually the people who have done things like that come over and are staggered by what they've done. If they're a young soul, they'll probably take a few months to sort over the sorrow and shock of it all, but if they're older they'll see it from both sides: they'll see the lessons they have to learn and they'll see the purpose they served in teaching those left behind the value of life and love as well as the lessons they helped with for those who had signed up to pass that way.

The goal for every one of us is to let go of fear and the idea of ownership of physical things, so it all serves a purpose (albeit one that's very hard to look at from a mortal perspective, I know). From what I have seen, it's people who get stuck on one small event like a perceived betrayal or their own guilt from betraying another. How could someone have done this to me seems to be the loop they get stuck on if they become malicious. Whereas how could I have done that tends to end in a seemingly endless black hole of sorrow and we would never let someone hurt that badly. We don't judge, remember that. You judge yourself.

In the case that one person horribly murdered another, it often works out in the next life that the murdered one is now a prison warden and the murderer a prisoner, or perhaps the murdered has become a junkie and the murderer is the person who saves them. People work out their debts between themselves. The only person who will ever truly break you, so to speak, is you.

The other things I wanted to say was regarding how I referred to those dark malicious things as demons. They are what people call demons, I think, those shadowy figures and those unexplained things that happen to people in their homes that seem to go beyond that of just a bump in the night. They might send awful images when you close your eyes and you're too tired to protect yourself, but they tend to be quickly taken care of in one manner or another. It might just be reinforced guards on our side, or it could be what I discussed above. Either way, remember the grass blade in the field – it's rarer than rare. What you see in movies regarding exorcisms and the like are not these things. They won't cause you to speak in tongues and for your head to twist around in circles; they couldn't even do that if they tried. Demons are, for our purposes of discussion, just deeply misguided souls that don't necessarily think of themselves as human any longer and may be able to toss your lamp on the carpet. If you ever find yourself confronted with such a thing, tap into the light that is available to you at all times and use it to ground yourself. You won't be harmed, because all it is trying to do is isolate you in the same way that it has done to itself, so that you are caught by fear of what you could lose. You can't lose anything, it's a part of you inasmuch as it can be.

Finally, if you ever run into something that you think is a ghost, remind it to tap into the infinity that it should have remembered long before. Encourage it to think of itself in other lifetimes. Ask it things like, remember when you were a man, if it is a woman, or remember when you were very old, if it is young. If it responds with confusion, you may have a chance at helping it cross. If there is no response, it is likely just a memory loop. Hope this helps!

On Accessing the Source

THERE ARE MULTIPLE WAYS TO access the infinity that exists beyond the borders of your physical form. All of them relate to blurring or removing those borders, at least in the sense of the ones you have imposed yourself on your soul. Depending on the type of person you are this can take many forms, for example beautiful music that makes your soul take flight, or a series of peaceful images. The music side is very simple: find a piece of music that makes you feel like more than yourself and try to join it. Seriously, attempt to become one with that sound for it is more than you in your singular form. With practice it should cause the edges of your non-corporeal being to vibrate and you may know the Source yourself. I have never in any of my lifetimes been a great composer, but it seems to me that in certain cases songwriters are attempting to access the divine and providing a pathway for others in which to accomplish this.

So, the other options. It really depends on how you feel about the concept of infinity. Ask yourself: what does everything in existence look like all at once? What does time look like? People might say it is the colour white, it may be the colour black. It might be pure light. It may spread across their entire vision, but that's often too much for people to start out with. Instead I try and suggest to people that they picture something vast, such as the ocean or all of the sand in a desert. Instead of meditating on the concept of nothingness, which is often frustrating for the human mind, try and conjure some mental waves that flow in and out endlessly. Listen to them, make them as clear as you can. Continue on that path until your mind has relaxed and then ask your question. There's always a question. The answer should come both from without and within simultaneously, and then you know that you have tapped into the Source in some small way.

For the purposes of alternate options, let me briefly describe the sand thing. I suggest picturing a single patch of sand in the desert and focusing on it until you can make out all the individual grains of sand, one by one by one. Once you can do that, tilt your mental camera outwards so that you can see the dunes stretching out ceaselessly into the distance. Think on that. Realize that if you are a grain of sand in that desert you are also that desert. You are more than you think you are and it is all available to you, always. Ask your question.

About Mystics

I WAS ASKED TO SPEAK on this topic, but I'm not sure that I agree with the term. To assume that some people are mystics and some are not is to go against the idea that we are all everything at once and all capable of all things. I will discuss it under the definition that some people return to the physical form in order to teach. The arrangement for the great teachers comes both from and is of a higher level than I exist on, that is to say maybe four or five levels above regular humanhood. I think they paint history, so to speak. From my understanding, one of them agrees with the other ones of their level and chooses to come onto the earth to make a point. It is not a point that hasn't been made before, however.

All the great teachers preach of love, joy and detachment from physical things. They don't even have to believe in the divine to teach this. Anyone who professes something else is a charlatan, pure and simple. It sounds harsh, but if you trust me to accept that pure joy and the love that lends itself to that emotion — to that energy — is the pinnacle of existence, you must trust that anything less than that is falsehood. It also means that you should not fear these people, nor hate them or resent them, because they are yourselves. Seek only your own enlightenment and pass on what you know to those who wish to know it.

So why do mystics appear here and there? Well, one surprising side effect that you may have noticed by now is polarization. Remember when I said that some people have the uncomfortable job of providing difficult lessons for others? Think of how religion often creates conflict. The role of a great teacher is two-fold: to provide a path of enlightenment for some, the only path of enlightenment presented in various forms, while the other one is to ensure a certain amount of conflict happens so that people can hopefully one day be separated from their fear and baseness. Can you imagine passing over and realizing that your zealousness that resulted in estrangement or death was the exact opposite of the goal you were trying to reach? It's quite an eye opener. It's one that all of us go through via different pathways. I think the point, at the heart of it all, is that they create discussion. They create conflict and discord as well as beautiful expressions of human nature, but in the end what they do is provide people with a direction.

If great teachers did not exist, we would be nothing more than animals scrounging for food and rutting against one another, never knowing that it is closer than fighting about land and food and ownership over each other, isn't it? It's a start at least.

On the Crest of a Spiritual Wave

SPEAKING OF GREAT TEACHERS, ANOTHER one is coming. I feel like it is another man, which is doubtless irritating to those of you who would like to see a woman in that role, but when I speak of him I want to say him and that's all I know. I think people will recognize him. I don't think he has been born yet. He is not a man of a church in the sense of buildings of glass, not a suit-wearing preacher type. He is of the outdoors, more of what you would picture as a yogi, I suppose. Perhaps not that ascetic. He speaks of a middle road insofar as there should be no path to enlightenment except the pursuit of love. He says things like the middle road is the place not to stray from, that hatred is one side and a life without spirituality is on the other. People are being prepared right now to listen to him. I think that if we are able to be born as young souls into an already enlightened world, the thoughts that come forth from that could be some beautiful, incredible things.

I say that we are part of an infinite and yet singular universe, and if you look around yourself at this moment you know that this is not every possibility that exists. There are things yet to come, things that come from the minds of people and are manifested in wonderful ways. I look forward to that existence and I do marvel at the way the world unfolds. Mind you, I see beauty in suffering too only because great moments of knowing and of stripping away of tiny minds and fears come from this. We will have greatness, but it is always a work in progress that comes from learning lessons. People do not learn without first being taught to yearn for something better. But, we will have it. You are all being prepared to head in that direction, perhaps for an age of enlightenment, as people like to call them. You may call this past century the dark ages in the future for all that came of it – great medical advancements came on the backs of pestilence and war, and scientific breakthroughs and discoveries often came while we wallowed in our own filth. I did not exist in a physical body in the past century, but I found it very overwhelming in both an awful and a good way. The sheer scale of events of the twentieth century set up the crest for this spiritual wave. Like an earthquake paves the way for a tsunami, it must be on a grand scale for things to really take hold. Without appalling conditions there can be no revolution.

One of the major features of this wave will be the linking of minds. I really must say at this point that I hate speaking in the future tense because it sounds like some sort of prediction and I don't view life in terms of a past-present-future timeline, so when I use the word will you please remember that it is against my will. Then again, to put things into sentence form needs must. Bear with me. As I say, the linking of minds. I taught you earlier how to break down the barriers that keep your mind confined to your own little vessel, which means that you are able to tap into the energy of the Source itself and the energy of all things. In the event that a great number of people perform this act together and reach out into the universe, they will be able to link metaphysical hands. Just imagine the things that could be accomplished by that! It's quite incredible, isn't it? I picture it as a combative action for all of the physical atrocities are carried out.

Many great voices throughout history have said variations of the saying that the mind is mightier than the sword. From sages to prophets to warlords, they have all agreed on this point with good reason. The only way to defeat fear is with your mind, and thus all of the bad things that come from fear must also be defeated that way.

In order to move beyond the horrors of war the linking of minds is necessary, and that's how it will be accomplished. In some ways this is a metaphor for a global shift in civilization, but in other ways it is absolutely literal. If you have ever felt that the way you approached a day affected its outcome, think of seven billion people changing their approach to the day. Think of even half of those people and the way that, if they are tapped directly into the energy fields that form the world, they could affect the fabric of reality. They could and should want to do this, both for those who are struggling around them and for the sake of themselves. It could be beautiful. Just you wait. Wait and keep working on your meditations, and of course reach out to others. Make it as grand scale as you can imagine, but remember that it all starts with you. So long as you haven't let go of your own fears, you will run into conflict even as you try to do good. It all starts with you

Hierarchy within the Source

I suppose now is a good time to talk more about levels and their connection to the infinite. I won't say that just because you are alive it means you are at the lowest, most numerous level. I won't even say it's the biggest, only the most distinct level because people are at their most individual at the first step of the climbing process.

When I said earlier that people are born of the source, I said they are also their saddest or most base; by this I mean that their heads are full of the concept of individuality and that means that they have forgotten their origin completely. To feel that one is separated from the Source, from the thing that ties all things together and is indeed All Things, that is the greatest pain a person can know. That is the origin of fear and loss that I told you forms the basis for what we call evil. If you know that you are one with every rock and plant, every beam of light and every dark corner, you'll never fear any of it will you? If you knew that your very nature was part of all of nature, that there was nothing about you that could be unnatural, would you be comfortable with yourself? If you knew that all good things are based in an everlasting joy, that they are only manifestations of something so incomprehensibly perfect that even the worst times of our lives only serve to rediscover that perfection, would you be so distraught by life? That's where we all start out.

As we ascend within that level, we learn to let go of fear

and of temporal things, of our attachment to material goods as we let go of the ideas of possession and ownership. Aren't there more important things in the world? As we ascend we learn that judgement has no place with us, it is only a reflection of ourselves we compare. To compare oneself to another is to separate oneself from that person and assume that they are better than or a less than you. If we are all headed in the same direction and will all get there eventually, time ceases to hold meaning and therefore what we call evil should only be viewed as a roadblock in the path upwards.

People call this all sorts of things like Heaven and Nirvana and so on. Call it what you like, I don't really have a name for it. I suspect it must have all names, literally the name of everything that has ever existed or ever will exist, in order to be a proper infinity. It's nice to know that when everything in the universe is added up the equation equals something beautiful, don't you think?

So you've figured out that things are not as dire and small as you once made them out to be. You've let go of the physical, for the most part, and all the lessons you needed to learn from within a fleshly vessel have been learned. That's when you go to the next level, which I'm sure Jacob will tell me off for, but it seems like a very small leap. It's the level he's at, you may have guessed, and they are helpers on a small scale. I think I mentioned earlier that they tend to help around six people at a time, guiding them through their lives and assisting them with things like not dying before their time or having that extra little bit of strength to get through a painful experience.

They also work as what I would call beginner soul friends, ones that are perfectly able to help you if you have questions about your own life path and some of the things about life after passing. They have their own lessons to be learned from helping people – they get to observe, kind of like the way people talk about angels, and learn about the joy of the experience of living in that manner. I personally don't think it takes that long to process after you've gotten the hang of how all things lead to joy, but there are two problems with my judgment on that: first of all, time ceases to exist in a linear manner, so you can be in different places and times all at once.

I'm both proud and humbled to say I am of the third level. As I said earlier, we work on a slightly larger scale. I might have to deal with a bank robbery, for example, or a class trip. Let's take a look at the class trip scenario as a sort of case study for the first two levels above body-bound souls. Let's say there are twenty or thirty children in this class, and each person in this class has a Number 2 watching them with at least one-sixth of their attention depending on how large of an impact this trip is going to have on them. Each of these children has an eventual life goal, whether it be overcoming poverty or loyalty to their friends. Each Number 2 is observing their actions and will for the most part not need to step in, but they might do things like pull the back of one of the children's jackets if they would otherwise fall off the edge of the bluff they've gone to see. They might also try and distract them if they aren't supposed to hear something the teachers are saying, but again only if this is going to have a large impact on their lives. The point is to let people do as much as they can by themselves, or else they aren't learning the lessons on their own merits.

So, this is perhaps a significant class trip. Someone is playing with matches they nicked from their parents and one of the rooms catches fire. There is one child in the bed away from the other children, lonely because they are excluded. How is the situation going to impact them? Are they going to run to the teachers first, and if so how will the other children react? Will they snub the lonely child further or be grateful that the lonely child saved them? Is anyone going to be hurt, even in a small way? Are any of the children going to have a phobia or an obsession with fire as a result? Are any of the parents going to sue the school and are any of the teachers supposed to lose their jobs as a result?

Number 2s know that their charges need things like these to nudge them in the direction of their life goals, but Number 3s look at the interlocking pieces like a puzzle and fit them in to accomplish as much of that as possible. Lonely child, for example, wasn't supposed to be a part of that scene so she wanders off to use the toilet. The child who started it is headed for a life of crime and this is the turning point, so that match definitely catches when it could have otherwise just been snuffed out with a wail of disappointment from the other kids. Little criminal's friends realize from this experience that perhaps being a cool kid isn't worth risking their lives for. The kids in the other rooms will tell their own children stories like this in the future when they're about to go on their own class trips. That's the kind of work I do.

For the purposes of full disclosure, I could also be considered level 4, but that's due to overlap and is maybe too complicated to explain here. Instead I'll just explain level 4 and maybe you can imagine how they might coincide. If Number 3s are like team leaders for Number 2s, then Number 4s are like team leaders for Number 3s. Think of a larger scale situation, like a plane crash or maybe a protest rally. There are hundreds, perhaps thousands of people involved in these situations. Each person has their watchers, followed by those who are going to be coordinating efforts for their particular group. In the example of a plane crash, one Number 3 might be assigned to each rescue crew involved or organizing the Number 2s to be there to guide those who will be crossing over. If there are to be any miracle survivors, they may be assigned to either a level 3 or a 4, depending on why they are surviving. If they end up writing a book about it or doing a talk show circuit, or else devoting their lives to airplane safety in the future and getting some laws changed, that'll be the job of a Number 4 to ensure. If they are surviving because they're supposed to be the parent of an important person in the future or they wrote an 'absolutely do not die prematurely' clause into their life contract because they've earned it, their survival will be signed off on by a level 3. Hopefully this gives you some idea of how it works.

Mainly the difference between a level 4 and a level 3 is the scale on which they work. Number 4's coordinate things that make the national news, but will be a footnote in history in the future. Awful as it is to admit it, most plane crashes are big news for the months following and are reviewed at the end of the year, but may not be recalled in great detail in the years to come. If it is something that people will make movies about and refer to when talking about examples of famous crashes, that is the work of a Number 5.

Recall that as we are ascending the hierarchy we are moving farther away from the concept of a vessel and therefore a human form, so it gets more and more difficult for high level beings to present themselves in a manner that makes sense to the human mind. When they descend without a human form people tend to call them miracles, apparitions of saints and angels and other deities. The reason they appear on the earth from time to time is to speak to prophets who will be used to teach on a grand scale in the future, or sometimes Number 6 may be used in these events. You can be sure that every great religious figure in history, the ones who actually founded major religions, were visited or maybe even were a level 5 or 6.

Yes, it is possible for such people to take human form in the most important situations, but such people tend to be jaw dropping and awe inspiring. They don't seem human, they seem to have transcended humanity while still upon the earth. That's basically because they have. I imagine it's hard for them to even attempt to appear 'normal', but then again, they may not be concerned with such things either. It's not like time is something that bothers them much, so the comings and goings of life are likely not as earth-shattering for them.

I don't mean to say, when I'm explaining these things, that they are some how better than you. If there's one thing you take away from my writings, I hope it is that we are all connected and we are all the same, even if we are at different stages in the same journey. To judge in terms of better and worse is in itself a fallacy, so please just think of these higher levels as your brothers and sisters, who love you very much and are cheering you on no matter how well you do at this, just one of many lives. They serve the lower levels because they marvel in the beauty of wanting to transcend the trappings of human life.

Struggling to find that eternal joy is in itself a glorious thing, and its admiration and to some extent nostalgia that presses them to assist. Of course, they don't always just take care of dark things, they take care of the best things of human history as well. I think, and here it gets fuzzy, that level 7 takes care of abstract concepts like inspiration and anguish and how they can be translated into the physical plane so that they may be learned from. In this way Number 7s are also responsible for enduring events in human history; not the ones that last for decades but for centuries or millennia.

Imagine the scale you have to be able to see on in order to put together a puzzle that size! Think of all the millions, maybe even billions, of people who are to be affected by something like that. I think it must be marvellous.

After level 7 it heads upwards into even more abstract things that, even if I were able to clearly grasp it, I would be sorely pressed to explain to you in words. I think they go into the very fabric of reality on hundreds or thousands of levels above it, though the levels hardly look anything close to human anymore. They don't have the same sense of individuality anymore because they've learned more and more with each level that there is a sweet, perfect, all-encompassing oblivion at the end that they are both a part and the whole of at once. Names aren't a thing anymore, because you would have to name all things to call them by their true names, and I think they find beauty in things like the creation of stars. I'm closer to your level than I am to theirs, though I look forward to one day seeing the universe through eyes like that. At the end of it all is the Source, the pure joy and the infinity of all creation destined to be born of itself and return to itself. You are a child of that Source and you are that Source. It is likely that you have been born from that and returned to it before, but that previous journey and this one are not separate because nothing is separate. Try and wrap your head around that and you'll understand why I had to stop at level 7 or so.

Compatriots

I've been asked to speak a little bit about Clara (and other people, but I've chosen to speak about her more.) We were born as twin souls, as soulmates, many millennia ago. Now she occupies the same hierarchy level as I do and we do similar work, though she tends to never speak to the living. At least, I've never seen her speak to the living before. Sometimes she'll manage a little wave, but she's always been the retiring type. Very sweet, very kind, but not much of a talker, perhaps because I'm so proficient at it. We don't often work side by side on events, but I am always aware of what she is doing. We don't tend to speak to one another because speaking requires not knowing what the other person is thinking in order to have to communicate those details. I would say it is closer to a lava lamp, where we are aware of the formation of thoughts that don't come directly from us but arise within us much like those little blobs that stem from the whole and return to the whole, often prompting a response elsewhere within that whole.

We are, as I explained with soulmates earlier, essentially occupying the same space. We're beyond being able to move through one another's energy so much as we can't tell the difference between one another's energy. Still, there is some semblance of conjecture and response that exists between us and that is why I call her Clara and not also James.

I also call her Clara because I'm an old softy and I loved when she was called Clara, so it's more for my own selfish benefit than any other reason. To me she is the imprint, the soul, that was known as Clara in one lifetime but is very much more than that. I would recognize her in any form, male or female, young or old, healthy or not, sane or not. And I would always want her with me. I also want to say all of this because it means I trust her implicitly and I have never questioned her decisions on the current level we occupy, even though I often did when we were young and encased in bodies. I've come to think that one can't make a wrong decision or a right decision much, only a decision. It may transpire to be a mistake in the future, but it was still the only decision one could have made. She assists me in my job by teaching me about such things, because I can view her in a better light than I view myself and then apply the same lessons to my own work. She is the happy friction I spoke of when discussing the birth of souls, and so I think that is the most essential function of a soul mate: to teach and help each other grow.

Other people that may be considered part of my circle are Jacob, who I have mentioned is a level 2. I think he is currently waiting to ascend by some choice of his own. He needs to be better grounded to the earth still – and yes, one may choose when they want to ascend if they have completed all metaphysical requirements of that ascension. We were born at a very similar time as well and through some meeting of minds found ourselves choosing lifetimes together, planning lessons and grievances in harmony with the other. We fought in the same wars and raised children together, beat one another to a pulp and – I am hesitant to admit – were lovers as well. It was a very awkward lifetime and she, at the time, decided I was too maddening for words.

That is another point of soul mates, they are not always born to be in love. In order to learn all the aspects of the human condition it's very narrow to stick to romantic interaction. Clara, for example, has been my child and my brother, my mother, my father, once my cousin and even my jailor. In such lifetimes it is the people you consider part of your circle who often play other people in your family or your life. Over thousands of years, the variations are numerous. Most souls will prefer one gender to another, but some flip back and forth every other lifetime. Some soul mates will marry one another and live happily ever after, while others will get into horrendous fights that last several lifetimes. It seems strange, but there is a lesson to be learned in all of it. There are only nigh infinite paths to get there. Just remember that if there is someone who you can't forget, whether for better or worse, they were probably important to you in another way in a previous life. We recognize one another whether we choose to admit it or not.

Anyone else mentioned in this book who is from this side was once someone I knew in living life, though Jacob is my closest friend and Clara is more to me than words can say. If you are looking for a challenge, think of the people you care about the most and try to figure out what other roles they have played in your past lives. You can also look at the people who you like the least and figure out how they slighted you in the past.

Friends, because that's what they must have been to you in order for them to speak to you like that. I like the reference and it seems the most accurate description so far.

Souls

SOUL FRIENDS THAT ARE DIFFICULT to get a read on are either not very close to you as souls or are being blocked by some memory that you don't want to delve into, such as a traumatic death or some previous transgression. Try to remember if there are any good things about this person, rather than focusing on a single event. Even if you can't recall the event itself, you'll be able to feel an uncomfortable tugging that seems to have a sole anchor, which suggests you've narrowed your relationship with this soul friend to one bad experience and that is ignoring what you've been to one another on the whole. If you are still unable to get past it at that point simply send them on their way with apologies and try to sort it out between you after you pass. As I said, there are plenty of people who you can connect with because you've likely had that many lifetimes. I can't imagine any brand-new souls would be reading this book because they're often too preoccupied with base things rather than learning and seeking enlightenment. To answer another unasked question, new souls are born every day even now, and despite what some might have you believe there is no limit to the number of souls that can be born.

On the other hand, some people are indeed born without souls (though I am reluctant to call them people). I want to say it is a fairly rare case, but it tends to be what people call pure evil when it happens. There is no compassion, no remorse, no ambition and certainly no rhyme or reason to their actions.

The difference between someone who has come back to commit evil deeds or someone who has fallen off the path and begun to commit evil deeds versus a body without a soul is characterized by motivation. Someone who has done awful things from their youngest days without a reason beyond wanting to may not have a soul. From time to time you'll hear this phrase in the news, that when the culprit is caught they have absolutely nothing to say for what they've done and can't acknowledge that it might have hurt someone else because the concept of pain doesn't occur to them. Often the concept of pain doesn't even sink in as applies to them physically and they won't process the idea of it beyond a very basic 'ouch', because pain has an emotional component in all cases where a soul is involved. Pain imprints are a learning exchange between the participants: the person who is inflicting it may have signed on to teach a lesson or they may be about to pay for their actions dearly, whereas the recipient also feels slighted, betrayed, robbed, incensed, compliant, baffled or any other emotion on the spectrum.

The point is that there is a motivation here, something deeper than the physical, that doesn't occur with those without a soul. They may look at the world through strictly scientific, childlike however intelligent they are, eyes – inflicting pain is at best to see what will come of it.

I emphasize this point because in the rare case that a body is born without a soul, it more or less always culminates in violence. Other sorts of crimes, such as stealing, carry the desire to live in comfort or luxury. The soulless tend to be unconcerned with much more than the basic functions of life – as long as they have clothes, a place to stay, something to eat and drink, they don't care much for anything else.

Why does this happen, I'm sure you're wondering. The tricky thing is that the soul enters the body at a very specific moment and has to have been signed up for the journey. All things crossed and dotted, the soul enters the baby and it is born with the two attached. Sometimes the attachment doesn't occur and the soul floats back off into the atmosphere, so to speak, or sometimes they miss their opening.

Again, this is an extremely rare situation so please don't think this is an everyday thing – it's just that I want to answer as many questions that people might have as possible. As to why the people on my side don't just, for lack of a better word, reap the soulless beings that walk about, it's more to do with the parents than anything else. It tends to be that the parents of that child signed on for learning via parenting and the death of that child would hinder their path too much. From there the body wandering free has to be monitored closely because in theory anything they do could interfere with the pattern, with the design of things. A lot of negotiating goes on when bad things occur and I suspect in the end of it even these mishaps are worked into the shape of things, but I am no orchestrator, only one who carries out and can make some minor judgement calls.

On Books of Faith

EVERY BOOK OF FAITH WAS written by, necessarily, people on Earth. Each one of them has acquired a sort of mythology over that time that sometimes suggests they weren't of the earth. If the book was purported to be written with the help of angels, well, we now know what angels are. For events as massive as a religion with millions, perhaps billions, of followers, it would require at least a level six, more likely a seven or an eight to order its creation. Interestingly though, it wouldn't be the level six who gave the authors the information but rather a three or a four. Instead, the permission would be given by higher beings who will see the far-reaching effects of creating such a book and orchestrate its creation accordingly. What I want to say is rather than the books themselves we should look at the way they were spread in order to make them popular. Rather than the words in them we should look at the way they have been used as tools of change both good and bad. The words contained in them are nothing that are not contained in old adages passed down from generation to generation or said by a wise old person in your neighbourhood who has things figured out pretty clearly. Every book of faith that forms the centre of a major religion should be viewed as the catalyst of a movement rather than a book of all the answers.

This is not to say that there isn't truth in them; as I say there is. It's just that the truth in them is also available to you as easily as if you were to speak to God or the Source or anyone on our side. Moreover, the problem with deciding that all of the answers are in a piece of literature means that those answers don't come from you, and there is no way to teach people the actual truth of something they are told. They can be directed towards that nugget of enlightenment but not persuaded to take it; only they themselves can do that. Thirdly, a person's path to enlightenment takes many shapes and is, as far as I know, never the same way twice. It generally takes a large number of rebirths (though some have been known to make massive leaps in the space of one lifetime) and picking and choosing the ways to get there. We do that on our own.

I'd like to impress upon you that anyone that uses a book as a substitute for their own thoughts and analysis is about as far away from enlightenment as they can get. Either they are not strong enough to take the next step, of moulding what they've read into their own world view instead of taking it verbatim, or they took too much on in this life and it's the words of someone who lived thousands or hundreds of years ago that offer them the crutch they need to keep on 'til the end of this life. Either way, don't be too concerned with them unless they're dangerous – and then be even less concerned, because a man with a broken leg will hang onto that crutch for dear life. I mean to say you won't change them and they won't be changed of their own volition either. You have to focus on the things you can control. If you try to get into a fight with such people, it will only serve to distract you from the harder task of bringing yourself towards your own truths.

So, back to the books. Anything that isn't written regarding joy or love or the letting go of material things can immediately be tossed out the door. Thankfully whichever book you choose to subscribe to (if any) will always contain a little bit of those points. Kindness to others, do unto others as you would unto yourself – those are the good bits. I'll say it again: you are the universe. That's not just some sort of inspirational speech, so you can imagine how important a statement like that is. Anything beyond that is just clutter and I venture to say it wasn't written by the authors themselves. Remember what I told you? They are catalysts of movement rather than books of answers.

It's much more valuable from a 'me vs. the universe' standpoint to look at what the books of faith have accomplished over their history rather than what is contained in them. To look at the beautiful works of art that they have inspired, or the bloody wars and the unrelenting judgment that has spread from them – that is a much better portrait of human nature than what is included in these works. In a religious song, we understand that people will always be seeking what is above them spiritually, striving to be better. We learn that those things are possible too, as I'm sure you've noticed when your soul resonates while listening to ones that really speak to you. We understand that the best way for a person to feel is enveloped in love, connected to the Source. We look at incredible works of art and we understand that we can be inspired by someone else's path to enlightenment, that we are all able to inspire and push each other towards these goals – we realise that we can speak to each other without words and without even living in the same time period and still reach the same conclusions.

On the other hand, we can look at the wars and violence, the discrimination and pain that has been done in the name of these books. Yes, I mean every single one of them. Even the – ? Yes, even that one. There has never been a book of faith in human history that has not caused the shed of blood and tears. They are the result of the laws contained in these books. These are the things that people argue over. In their purest form (and as far as I am aware the way they were written before other people got their hands on them and added things that could be used to control their society) these books were explanations, not rules. There should never be a law or a rule in a book of faith, and if there is? I personally wouldn't put much credence in it. The laws of the universe at large will never be written down, only the rules of society in a given time period.

Over the years I spent in living vessels I was the member of a great many religions and sometimes none formally, but I was always connected spiritually to the greater universe in some way. I think it's actually dangerous not to, because no matter how wonderfully a person lives their life if they are convinced that all they are is stuck in a single body, they're missing a massive part of the big picture. That worries me a little, but so long as they are going about doing kind things and searching for the best way to be a good person, how they want to get there is up to them. As soon as you start trying to tell another person how to connect with the Source, you've got problems on both sides – resentment on one and a manifestation of that ownership thing I spoke of earlier that is the root of evil. To assume that you know better than another person, to force them to think the way you want them to, is a sort of ownership, a slavery of that other person, and so it cannot have any positive outcome. Would you be pleased to say you broke a person?

Incidentally, I was born into the same religion hundreds of years apart on a variety of occasions as well. Can you imagine how differently interpreted the same book was over those many years? The only thing recognizable between them was that same message that endured over time, the only message that was passed on by the Source in the first place. Everything else, all those laws and rules, were ignored or twisted or focused on in great detail depending on the moral slant of society and politics at the time. Truth in its most intrinsic form never alters.

In conclusion to this part, I think every book of faith has its gems and that each of them has sand to wade through in order to get there. I don't think one book is better or worse than another, because I see the bad bits as things to be ignored and not worth anyone's time, but the good bits as always worthwhile. So long as you keep your eyes on the prize, read all of them or none of them or whichever one you like. Once again, I emphasize that I do not value one religion over another, but rather love the idea of religion in general as it seeks to connect and overcome the limitations of the human body and the constraints it places on the soul.

On a completely personal note, the reason I am called James is because I finished my last life in a Christian environment, so my most recent memories of living life may be coloured by that. (Author's note: James said as an aside that because of that he likes Song of Songs in the Bible because there's nothing but love contained in it. Also, Ombra Mai Fu by Handel was playing in my head towards the end of this section.)

The Reality of Our World

LET'S START THIS OFF BY thinking about the nature of time. If we assume that the Source is infinite and the universe is infinite, then we must also accept that all things exist simultaneously. If that's too much for you, try "the idea of all things exists simultaneously". Now think of what scientists say about the life cycle of the planet you are living on and tell me if it is going to exist forever. It cannot, just as all living things cannot. On the other hand, it is a soul which will one day be transformed into a greater thing; a different thing.

When people talk about the soul of the Earth, they are not just paying lip service. Every single thing contains what someone might consider to be a soul, because everything is composed of the same everything from which we are born (i.e. thoughts, simply put). The physical manifestation of a thing is no different than the physical manifestation of ourselves, which is thoughts put into action. You can do a great number of things to be a Creator in your own right, but more about that later. For now, I want to focus on the things that are in physical existence.

Difficult as it is to explain, there both are and are not alien worlds. They exist to teach us and yet they are us, which is a story way above my pay grade. Okay, so – people learn from mirrors. Even when a soul is born it needs a mirror to figure its way into existence. Therefore, the idea of aliens as well as the reality of them are both mirrors in that they serve to teach us. However, when we consider time as being non-linear we can also say those aliens are us, because if they have souls then they must have been born from the same pool as we were. We must accept this to be true because the pool we were born from is the Source, aka infinity, and because once we are returned to the source we will be born again of our own volition, perhaps not on this Earth.

Perhaps at that time this planet will not be hospitable to life, having reached the end of its life cycle and returned to the Source itself. And yes, just as with humans, it is possible for the husk to remain while the soul heads elsewhere. Anyway, alien worlds are just us in disguise. If we were ever to reach them I think certain other rules of reality would come into play, but as it stands planets of a similar nature to ours will contain similar life forms, and because time is completely arbitrary they may not technically exist at the same time as we do.

An easy way to check for this is to compare someone on the opposite side of the world: here may be day while there is night, they have technically lived through the hours we are living or vice versa and yet we exist simultaneously and are able to talk to one another on the phone etc. The very definition of time itself has to keep being adjusted to fit people's needs and increased understanding of the Earth (of reality?) but I really wish they'd just do away with it. Even time itself is a mirror, you know – one by which people can measure themselves. They can get sad at a missed birthday or excited at having run faster than ever before, but the limitations of time mean limitations to what we believe we are able to do. I really dislike it, and I used to own a lot of pocket watches.

Just a bit more about life: all things are composed of energy, the likes of which can be used to form anything. Human souls follow a human path, dog souls follow a dog path, rock souls follow a rock path and so on. The definition of soul is quite sketchy at that point though, because they don't represent the same sort of thing that we do.

Dogs, for one, are able to learn lessons and think things through but on a much tighter scale. Think of how some dogs are quiet and wise and others are willing to chew on every item on your house or will not stop barking in the early hours of a Sunday morning. This is the dog equivalent of an old soul and a young soul. Furthermore, some dogs are able to be born into a sad scenario of abuse while others live on the laps of celebrities depending on what they choose to learn. Dogs too are reborn until they reach the pinnacle of their understanding and then, as far as I am aware, they return to the source directly (or at least more directly than we do, definitely) to return as whatever their little bit of infinity chooses to be next time. Could be a human, could be a dolphin, could be a leaf on a tree – the point is that they finish their necessary life cycle and return to the Source of all ideas and possibilities and from there another idea is born.

Rocks? I have no idea what the life cycle of a rock is except that they contain energy that can be manipulated and vibrated; perhaps to a rock the correct series of vibrations or finding the correct manifestation of its own energy is the life cycle. Some rocks are older than others and some rocks have transformed into beautiful shapes all naturally occurring. We always think of the water as having shaped the rock and are all in awe of water, but what if we also considered that the rocks chose that for themselves as well? No two rocks are exactly the same, after all.

Reaching Life Goals

So that one lifetime I decided to share with you, one lifetime I am not particularly proud of, counted in the end. I believe that because the circumstances around me eased up and I was able to manage at least a half-smile here and there in the years before I died that I just squeaked by on the pass or fail scale. It didn't really count as a victory anyway, although Clara's unwavering loyalty counted far better towards her so-called final score. She never gave up or resented me in spite of how badly she must have also been hurting for the duration of that lifetime. What I mean to say is that you absolutely can and probably have failed at life, or rather fail at the goal you assigned to yourself.

I'm not going back and talking about suicide, not at all. I want to say that you can without a doubt die as an elderly person without ever having accomplished what you set out to do when you signed up for this life. The best way to figure out where you stand in terms of this is to figure out what the most awful thing that has happened to you thus far is and how it has changed your life. If you don't feel like you've had anything particularly awful happen to you, don't just assume that it is coming. You might have merely signed up for a fairly trauma-free life. On the other hand, if you can name an event that hurt you very badly, it is probably the key to how you are supposed to change and grow.

As an example, we could consider someone who came from a broken home and how they are supposed to learn not to repeat their parents' mistakes. Alternately they may be destined to mentor another child from a broken home or become a social worker. We could consider someone who finds it difficult to let go of the rage or the sadness related to those events or even someone who is supposed to learn to trust.

Even things like someone who grew up with very little money – often the goal in these cases is to figure out how not to let it dominate your life. You may become extremely rich and obsessed with making more money (be it greed or paranoia that drives you to it) or you may remain poor and be obsessed with how little you have, in turn becoming bitter and complacent. If you recall my chattering's on the subject of possession and ownership, you'll know that both of these paths are failures. You may end up stuck in complete mediocrity, never seeming to get ahead because you can't let go of your fear and take the risks that you were meant to take, to which my advice is: Does it feel right? Trust that! Is it going to kill you? If not, go for it! If it might but you will still be proud of yourself if it does, you might have to risk it anyway. If you would admire someone like you who did the same thing and if you would consider them a hero, you should absolutely head in that direction. Do things that matter. If you can't figure out what matters, see my explanations on how to meditate and its purpose. When your brain isn't cluttered by pettiness and present tense it's a lot easier to see the things you're supposed to see.

Furthermore, I'd like to tell you to pay attention. One of the worst things people do to sabotage themselves is consider any of it wasted time or useless. If you are getting something out of it, even if it's not what you thought you wanted to get out of it, it's useful. Say you go to a concert and you're interested in seeing the headliner so you ignore the opening act in favour of getting another drink. It's very common for life to do something like set you up at a party, months down the road, and the person you fall in love with at first sight or your future business partner will ask you if you've ever heard of that opening act. Life itself is trying to see if you're paying attention and it definitely wants to see what you can make out of these tiny everyday coincidences, which is not going to be much if you weren't watching when they were taking place. More than live deeply I would suggest to live broadly; in other words, see the big picture with your human senses and take it into the limitless self that you possess. Figure it all out to the best of your capacity and don't just live on the surface. Your days don't have to be exciting and they don't have to be anything anyone else tells you they should be, but they absolutely have to matter.

If, on the other hand, you do fail at a lifetime remember that it happens to every single one of us no matter how all-knowing and amazing they seem now. All of the great figures in history and myth were once crying over their stupid potatoes like I once was, but after they passed they took what they could glean from the pieces and they used it to try again only better. There's no time limit because there is no time, remember? All things are accomplished in all time. Just do your best and realize that your best is enough for the universe, no matter what any other living being thinks of it.

Auras

AURAS, AND BY EXTENSION HALOS, are representations of energy in the form of light. There are people who can see them with little difficulty, but most of them have to make a concerted effort to see that they're there. There are two types of auras as well, and I feel that the term halo should be used interchangeably with aura. Basically, when you reside within a human vessel (or any vessel), your body doesn't play by the same rules as your soul does. If the skin were a solid line that blocked all things out it wouldn't be useful because the soul could not connect with the rest of the universe. The soul has to vibrate beyond the limits of the human body because it needs to reach out to the energy of everything around it. This isn't some sort of saccharine platitude but genuinely true – if you've ever needed to do something you thought you couldn't possibly, you borrowed the energy of the universe around you to accomplish it.

This thing we call luck is, apart from the events orchestrated by your watchers, essentially tapping into the Source and making it work for you. If you've ever heard stories of men and women lifting impossible objects in a time of dire need or boarding a train they shouldn't have been able to make, that's reaching out and manipulating external energy. (Again, I say external but to me there is very little difference. There are only as many barriers as we ourselves create.)

So, your soul spreads beyond the limits of your physical body by just a little bit on a normal basis and that is why skin itself is semi-permeable. As I said earlier on, rocks are capable of having a say in their own form so why wouldn't human design work on a similar basis? Even on an evolutionary scale we know this to be true, and here's a meditation point: why do people have opposable thumbs? Why are they the height they are? What function does this serve our spiritual evolution? And if you get through that point you can start imagining a white light painting the edges of the body all over, maybe just the width of a finger or two to start.

I say white because, well, white is meant to be all of the colours combined and that makes it not only easy to explain but it also describes pure energy. Auras are famously capable of being a variety of colours as well, but to me that suggests an imbalance. This is not to say that an imbalance in the soul's colour is necessarily a bad thing, just that it is currently geared towards certain emotions or outcomes. You can even adjust the colour of your own aura through strongly weighted thoughts or feelings and if you practice at it you can extend your soul further than those one or two inches and tap in further.

Wouldn't that be dangerous or scary, you might ask. It could even be painful, you may be thinking, to keep one's soul that far beyond the safety of the body, but that's not true. Your soul is still deeply rooted within you, it's just that it is able to tap into the infinite energy that exists around it. The only side effects tend to be being less bothered by trivial things and perhaps less concern about the passage of time on a daily basis. I don't see how that's a bad thing, personally. It's not exhausting either because it's a bit like a tree spreading its branches so that it gets more of the sunlight. In turn the tree can grow bigger, but is always taking in energy with which to do so and therefore not exhausting its stores. Sunlight,

I find, is a good metaphor for the Source as well: it's always in existence and an infinitely renewable resource (at least for the next good while!), and incidentally it is composed of that same white light that we are, while still being separable into a prism.

I don't want to give a specific colour guide based on what auras mean, only that bright/light colours are a good, healthy thing, dull colours are a bad (weak?) thing and that the intensity of the colour itself has more to do with how strongly a person is feeling at the time. The colours themselves do not have a set meaning because the colour-emotion connection is largely cultural, not a universal truth. Vivid colours can suggest anything from confidence to desperation, while the size of a person's projected aura relates to how willing they are to connect with the world around them. If you are in the habit of reading auras or trying to assist people based on them, take a small/thin aura as a sign of being closed off (open up, guys!) and a dimly coloured one as something akin to depression on a soul level. This might manifest in people stuck in a work rut, a dead-end marriage, struck by fatigue or feelings of being lost. If someone has an unbalanced colour too far in one direction, it may be useful to tell them to meditate on the opposite colour or a more neutral colour to help them feel better and get back on track.

As a side note, the reason religious figures are often depicted with halos is because they appear that way when they are extremely in tune with the Source and reaching out to greater knowledge so as to teach it to others. Their auras are that strong and that focused on drawing energy from the universe that they may appear as an honest-to-goodness halo, and white because white is the balance of all things, or else depicted as a golden-yellow related to wisdom or riches. Yellow equals wisdom and riches, you say? But James, didn't you just say the use of colour wasn't set in stone?

Well, when Soul Friends appear to people they use colours that they believe explain their personalities based on their experience of colours in life rather than an actual energy wavelength that they are operating on. Similarly, people may read auras in a colour that corresponds to how the person themselves feels and may not make complete sense to you. In other words, they choose the colours they project rather than your eyes choosing a colour to explain it to you. That's why reading auras can be tricky, and precisely why I chose to give a description of colour intensity rather than explain what the colours themselves might mean.

Energy Fields

I'M PLEASED THAT THIS TITLE sounds so science-fictiony, but what I want to talk about is something similar to ley lines. All landscapes on the earth are possessed of energy signatures that manifest in the shape of a grid. If you've ever seen a flight simulator on a computer you can probably imagine how this works. You can also train yourself to see them in the real world and they may assist you in navigating your daily life accordingly.

A lot of religions or philosophies are based on the use of energy manipulation, particularly in the East. Think Feng Shui, Tai Chi or Taoism, Onmyoudo and others. Energy lines are often the basis of superstition though, which can be seen in everything from the direction people pray in to the way that they are buried. Even though it has become cultural heritage, its roots are more intrinsic to the Earth itself. Let's start with the idea of windows and openings: ancient peoples wanted their dead to be buried in specific directions because they thought that certain directions contained gates – and they weren't wrong. More than the direction itself though, the point of being parallel and unobstructed by energy crossings was key.

Imagine a tic-tac-toe/noughts and crosses board made of real walls taller than yourself. You're in the centre and you want to escape: do you go through the corners or through one of the walls?

Furthermore, are you going to choose to spin around and smash the wall behind you, one of the ones to your sides, or are you more likely to go forward? That's why graves were positioned that way, although in theory the soul should have already departed. It wasn't a conscious choice so much as an innate understanding of energy pathways and the desire to allow their loved ones to reach their rest as quickly as possible.

This concept of allowing energy to travel more freely also carried forward to the placement of objects in homes and businesses, to auspicious pathways and even to places being declared cursed. As I told you in previous entries, places with a great deal of tragedy can end up with so-called bad energy that attracts more of the same. This tends to be because the gridwork in that area is out of tune or warped – and ancient humans knew that as well. That's why they buried things in their walls and floors or placed their religious icons facing certain directions, in an effort to repair that frayed energy.

In a place with good energy, you should feel free to tap into it as much as possible and to thrive from it, but if you make the mistake of reaching out too much in an area with bad vibes you run the risk of becoming entangled in it. Incidentally, the reason people say 'bad vibes' and 'good vibes' is related to the vibration of those energy fields. The collective subconscious often picks up on these things and creates phrases that they don't realise have a deeper meaning. If you have ever entered an area that felt 'dark' and come away feeling like you're covered in cobwebs, you'll understand what I mean by becoming wrapped up in off energy.

I'd like to say that you can use your own energy to reverse the problem in a difficult area, but first you need to be able to see those energy lines. It's very unlikely but not impossible to see them with the naked eye, so let's start with meditation to get us there. Go physically to a place that you always feel comfortable in and close your eyes. A quiet place is ideal to start with and somewhere in nature, because things grow according to the energy lines without fuss but when humans build, they often forget to take these lines into account. If you've ever seen a plant grow through the cracks of the pavement, you've witnessed a particularly rich knot of energy that humans completely missed out on harnessing. I guarantee that if they'd put a coffee machine there, it would have made the most excellent coffee, or if they'd placed a bench there it would have seen the most beautiful first kisses and happy children playing on it. Bit of a waste, don't you think?

So, you're out in nature, you're clearing your mind, you've closed your eyes. Picture a spot near your feet and imagine two lines spreading out into the distance, meeting other lines and criss-crossing into an endless grid. You can choose a colour for them if you find it easier, or you can visualize the lines in whatever other way allows you to see them. They aren't that small – they aren't infinitesimal or anything like that, but I haven't got an official measuring tape on the matter. I'd hazard a guess that they are between 6 and 9 feet per block, but if you actually measure them please let me know what you discover.

Look for consistency in the linework and try to discover spots that are weak, thin, frayed or on the opposite end thick and unmoving. The last ones of these are a bit clogged and will not respond well to 'tapping into', even though they might seem like they would be excellent for that purpose. We'll start with some perfectly normal lines and then we'll focus on reaching out and expanding the aura. Banish that fear you have about somehow stealing the energy or depleting it, because you and that energy are connected at the Source. You're trying to reach your full potential and you're assisting that line to do the same for itself, by being put to its best use to do great things. Try to do all of your business and personal dealings within areas of good energy lines and use them to the best outcomes you can. If you know a place to have bad energy lines, try to reschedule or relocate.

If you can't do either of those things, the first step is not to reach out too much. Being aware is the first step, because you can separate yourself rather than allowing the energy to mingle, which is more or less, default. If you discover these damaged spaces within your own home, there are plenty of texts that can help you with clearing the energy pathways so that they can return to normal. The only other thing you can do is go out there, collect lots of positive energy and push it out of yourself while making happy memories. It's not ideal, but it will certainly do the trick in a pinch. Remember that the lines will not heal themselves without energy pathways being cleared out so that good energy can travel in from other places. If you're donating those good vibrations, don't do it while standing on the lines themselves either; it can really backfire.

As always, you are welcome to take anything I say with a grain of salt. This journey is your journey and anything I tell you is only as good as you are able to understand it and apply it to your own advantage. If it conflicts with something in your belief system, by all means pick and choose and build your own understanding of the world. It's not possible – and I really stress this – it is not possible to fail completely and utterly so long as your goals are to be enlightened and to improve yourself, and to move away from hate and fear. You'll get there no matter what path you choose as long as it is your path.

On Limits

SPECIFICALLY, THE LIMITS OF THOSE on the other side, to start with. I was asked if we sleep or need other sorts of rest – the answer is no, because we haven't got physical bodies and are always tapped into the Source for that abundance of energy that allows us to carry out our tasks when they are needed. From time to time a difficult task may require reflection, at which point we do something I like to call 'turning off'. It's a bit like meditation in that we clear our minds and float in a sort of nothingness for some time in order to refresh our minds.

You might say "Aren't you nothing but a mind if you have no body? How can you do that?" And the truth of the matter is that we are two components at the very least: thoughts and the manifestations of those thoughts. We are able to physically affect the universe around us, not least of which we need to carry out our jobs, but we are also always manifesting ourselves through our thoughts. If I were to say, "Who are you?" to you, you might describe yourself by age, height, occupation or other relativity to people in your life but who are you when that's taken away from you? What if you were no longer in a body, not in a society, not a family member because you've had too many families for it to count, couldn't describe yourself via some hobby like painting because you don't have hands or paints or canvases anymore?

At that point, you are nothing at all if not your thoughts. That's why what you think even in the physical body may get buried under the outer shell but it's still changing things in the background, forming your personality and calling things to you. If I've just had to do something very difficult or hard (remember, many of us still have people we care about in living vessels and even if we don't, our motto is joy and love) I don't want it to become a stain on me and I do want to deal with the things I could be feeling from orchestrating a tragic event. I can go somewhere (although this is more of a non-physical state than a physical one) and reflect on it, and if it's too much I might turn off all thoughts for a little while and simply exist until I've got enough distance from the event. It's very similar to what people who have died painful or upsetting deaths often do as soon as they come to us, much as I described earlier.

I also want to say that it's not only tragic events that put us in that state, but also watching loved ones struggle or move on to happy things without us, that may require a time-out. I don't personally feel there's any shame in it and because time doesn't work the same way (or perhaps at all) here, there is no one accusing anyone else of having too many of these time-outs. If we did, we would already be failing at addressing our own problems. Until we reach the Source there is always room for growth and focusing on the struggles of others in anything that doesn't involve helping them up is turning away from one's own growth. I say this in the hopes that you too will realize you can and should take time for reflection, to work through your problems and not to wallow in them.

To accept that difficult things happen, that they doubtlessly happened for a yet unforeseen reason and that until you remove their grip, you will continue to be hindered by unresolved feelings. Furthermore, you are a manifestation of your thoughts and feelings, buried as they may be within your life and muffled by the goings-on of your body, therefore you should be mindful of who those thoughts are making you out to be. Not only who they're making you out to be but also what they may be bringing into your life. Make time to keep in touch with yourself.

Lastly, I want to impress an image on you that I think may help you to understand how important it is to check in on yourself from time to time. I won't advocate a particular schedule on how often you should do this reflection because there will be times you'll need more and times you'll need less, only I'll say in the period of 'not too late'. So, a particular person is having friends over to try their extra special secret recipe soup, which is currently on the stove. Three or four people come over and the host (or hostess) finds themselves chatting about work or school, about goings on with mutual friends etc. and in the meantime, one of the guests has spilled their drink everywhere so the host has to help them tidy up and another one asks if they can get some more of those finger sandwiches and a third wants to know the way to the toilet. Once all of that is sorted out you return to your soup only to find it has bubbled up so hard that it explodes all over yourself and your guests. Hot, smelly, painful and it may even stain. So, while comforting, guiding and contributing are all very important tasks, it doesn't stop your soup from boiling over and in the end keeping your precious people happy doesn't happen. In fact, an unwatched pot of internal goings-on ends up directly hurting those very people, so never say you're too busy. And if you noticed, one possible solution would be to turn off the heat under the pot and come back to it later – only unlike with cooking, turning off the soup would be less like shutting down emotionally and more like lying quietly and clearing your mind for a while, before turning the stove back on. Pretending you can leave your internal state alone until later, well – I hope you have a good towel.

The Human Potential for Suffering

I AM OFTEN ASKED HOW it is that we can live in a world where so many awful things happen both to us and to other people. I'm asked how with greed and violence human beings can stand to watch it happen (let alone the slightly more omniscient ones on our side). My first message to you is this: Can a light be stifled by darkness? If a light exists, does the darkness ever overwhelm it and put it out? Light, joy and love are the ultimate destination. We are all of us, every atom of every created thing, born of these and constructed from these.

We return to this. When we first generate into existence we are far from this and we are isolated because we cannot recall our connection to the greater being (for lack of a better word) that holds us all together. It makes sense because to first emerge from that vastness one has to define boundaries. It is the joy of rediscovering that there are no boundaries that makes us do it in the first place. The point is that there is no battle between light and darkness in this world, there is only darkness struggling to make an impact on the light. It will never triumph because that would negate the entire fabric of the universe. Tell me you are reassured by that!

The point of darkness, of violence and greed, is that it is born from fear and that misplaced idea that one can own a thing. I've said that before. However, it only exists to highlight just how wonderful life can be and just how glorious the living world can be. Do you remember every mildly pleasant day you've ever lived or do you remember the best times, the most important times? You may feel horror at the aftermath of an accident but you will also notice the way that people band together and help one another. You see acts of selflessness and kindness, of compassion and generosity. You see people fulfilling their destiny of remembering that borders do not exist outside our own constructs. For every awful thing that happens in the world, there are people who act as lights in that darkness. For every persecution there is a defender or a repenter, for every act of violence someone out there is standing up or cleaning up or healing. And that's why darkness can never even make a dent on the light, but it will always keep trying and all it will ever do is serve to make that light more radiant. For your own part, remember that every act of evil is a chance to be part of that beautiful opposite reaction. Even within a firework violence must occur as the chemicals and heat react, but from that is a thing of beauty and a beacon in the night. Whenever possible, even in the smallest way, please choose to be part of that beacon.

On Lowering Walls

SOME OF YOU MAY FIND the thought of lowering all of your walls terrifying – that the thought of letting other people in is difficult and dangerous. It's not, because fear and separation are the keys to everything bad that goes on within the world and on top of that, you can never lose yourself. You can bury it in other people, you can find it very difficult to see personally, but you can never, never lose it. For every stitch in that massive blanket I spoke of earlier, there is only one of them. If they were missing there would be a hole left behind. It wouldn't work. A stitch in this blanket may get frayed, twisted, misplaced – but it will never just disappear. It's always been there, it will always be there and if the blanket is remade it will be there again, whether in a similar form or an entirely new one.

You. Cannot. Lose. Yourself. If you feel like you can, or you could, or you have, you're lying to yourself. You're thinking far too externally. You cannot bury yourself under other people's messes and expect yourself not to be under there again when you go digging.

I know I speak entirely in metaphors but most of what I say can only be expressed in picture form, so please forgive me. I've got so much to say, too, that I often get side tracked. Please bear with me.

Let's say you hate your life at the moment. It's a struggle, you feel broken, you're in an unhappy relationship and no one listens to you. Does that mean you are incapable of doing all the things you need to? Are you incapable of success? A little voice inside you should be saying 'no' right about now. That's you! The real you that can't understand why you're doing this to yourself. You've surrounded yourself with people that don't fit you, stuck it out in a job that doesn't suit you, put up with things you shouldn't have put up with because you thought it was brave and self-sacrificing. Ha! There's the key – you've sacrificed yourself. And where has it got you? Nowhere you want to be! No one benefits when you sacrifice yourself. They benefit when you give of yourself, of your true self, and you put to work all the things you are truly meant to do for the sake of helping others.

If your children are treating you awfully, it's because you've held back in guiding them for their sake. Why would you have all the knowledge, life experience and gentle wisdom that exists inside you if not to help guide them? Just because you love them doesn't mean you have to be untrue to yourself – being truer to yourself can only help them by example, and by knowing what you were put on the Earth to do for them and why they chose to be born to you (or otherwise come into your life).

If your lover and you are unhappy, you're forcing something that is not true to you. You may be feeding into your insecurities or trying to be someone you're not, but the closer you get to finding the real you and bringing that out, the happier you'll both be. If you two are meant to be together, your partner will be charmed and comforted by the heart of the person they fell in love with. If you are meant to be with someone else, that should soon become infinitely clear to both of you. Furthermore, showing your true self gives others the courage to show theirs as well. Clearing away your distortions of them from your insides will also clear away some things for them as well. If we are too busy looking around us at the way other people see us, it has a profound effect on how much we bury our true sense of self as well. If we turn our external mirrors inwards and take away what we are projecting on the people in our lives, then that layer that buries their vision of themselves will go away as well. I hope this makes sense.

The same is true of work – if you aren't meant to be doing the job you are stuck in, you will only be fighting yourself in continuing at it. If you feel your job is what you were meant to do but are dismayed by your boss, it's because you've accepted his or her projections of who you are rather than sticking with who you really are. When one has a clear sense of self and accepts that it is impossible for that self to be stolen from them, there is no fear of lowering walls and there is no fear of being buried under other people's perceptions and projections of who we should be. If you want to improve everything in your life, dig through all the things that people have placed upon you and find out who you are. After that, take heart in who you are, be confident in that person and then lower your defenses so that other people can connect with you cleanly and lovingly. Voila, the key to a smooth and happy life.

On Giving Up

I WAS ASKED IN A roundabout way why people give up on fighting for love. It took me a moment to put it into words, but what I came up with was 'there is a difference between working at and fighting for'. I feel that this applies to not only matters of love but everything that is experienced in life. While working at something is a healthy and natural work in progress, people only fight for things they don't have. There is something very one-sided about having to fight for love. It's almost a contradiction, isn't it? So, my answer is essentially that people give up on fighting for love when they realize that it isn't supposed to be a battle, neither is it supposed to be one sided.

I'd like to extend this into matters of work and family. If your work life feels more like a struggle just to keep your head above the tide and you never seem to progress the way you want to, it's likely because you aren't supposed to be there. Some of you might say, "Work isn't supposed to be enjoyable! It's tough for everyone, but the truth is that there are just that many people in the world who haven't taken the steps they need to in order to thrive.

Consider these two people if you want to know the difference between 'working at' and 'fighting': both of them work long hours and sleep late on weekends. One of them says her work is extremely challenging and pushes her to the limit but she still finds it enjoyable. The other says she hates her boss, feels betrayed by her co-workers and can't seem to get promoted no matter how hard she works. Getting ready for work makes her feel like crying. The second is fighting for something that's never going to work because it's just not right, while the first is growing as a person, working to better herself and is benefitting her in the long run. If you feel like you are fighting life itself, it's time to give up and find a new path to follow no matter how scary it might be. After all, if you take the time to consider your situation you'll realize you don't have anything to lose, not when there's nothing you really want to keep. If you have nothing to lose, it can't possibly hurt to try something else.

Let's also consider the relationship between parent and child. I know that at various points in the development process children can be incredibly stressful. Parents can also be stressful to their kids, too. I'm happy to report that in the final lifetime I lived before I 'got promoted' I had many, many children – to the tune of 12! – and I had a good relationship with all of them. I can still remember all of them and the wonderful people they became. Special thanks to Clara for all of her efforts, of course. At that point I had learned something related to the topic of fighting for versus working at, though, so I'd like to share it with you if I may.

If you are a parent and you are frustrated with your child, as in extremely frustrated, and you can't understand how you spawned such a beast, it's likely that you are fighting for what you want rather than working with them to uncover who they are. It can be very hard to accept, but remember that there is no one on this planet who really wants to fail no matter what they project. Perhaps the child is 'fighting life' and your decision to force them down the path is only making things worse. I'm not saying at all that you should be easy on your children and never teach them to be strong, I'm only suggesting that you teach them to work at things instead of to fight them. Find every situation in which your child can thrive and help them to do so. When they don't excel, try and think of ways that they do excel and apply them to the situation. It's not as simple as struggling through for a cheap reward as many people think.

Indeed, as you may have read earlier the idea of struggling through a workday every day with only the goal of a cold beer does not contribute to your progress as a soul. Rather, learning from that workday and expanding as a person are the goals. If your work is a bitter pill that you must swallow in order to get to the ice cream, you're looking at the situation wrong. Why must one swallow bitter pills in the first place? Because they'll make you healthy! It's better to think 'Yes! I swallowed that pill, I worked hard and improved myself. This will not only benefit me in the future, but I have accomplished something and that's worthy of remembering.' The same is true for your children.

Guide your children to where they want to go naturally. If they are great lovers of books but need to get some exercise, offer to read to them while they jump rope or challenge them to talk about their favourite books while they hula hoop. If they are awful at math, consider who they are and how it might appeal to them. I'd rather not give any more examples than that because toys and other items are so fleeting. I want to say, in the most basic sense, that rather than giving them a break from themselves, help them to benefit by being more themselves. Do this for yourself as well, and remember that when you deal with them as adults as well.

For readers of this book who struggle with parental relationships, make sure first of 'working at' versus 'fighting for'. If you are approaching a difficult relationship in a healthy, open-minded manner but the other side is offering no concession, the situation is not only not your fault but perhaps not where your fate lies. Things that are meant to be come with effort but they come naturally, too. If you are still unsure as to whether your parental figure is willing to work at it, consider once again who they are and how you can help them be more themselves. Particularly if you have long had a good relationship with this person, you know well that they are capable of being kind, friendly or good-hearted. I think it would benefit you both if you look for ways to bring that out of them. Again, the goal is not to bring someone to your point of view but bring out the best in them. In our most essential form, we are all beings of love and joy and we shy away from fear, hate and ownership. We are all one and all on the same side in the ways that count. Everything else is just decoration.

So, when do you give up? When it's fighting for instead of working at, especially on a deeper level. Your intuition will tell you which it is if you let it.

Compassion

For all that I speak of the bigger picture and the mutability of or the transience of pain, we are not immune to your suffering. It's not to say that we don't know what it's like or how awful it is to lose someone; after all, in a lot of cases it's you we've lost. But there's the thing: we're still around and we know it, but we struggle to watch you doubt and wonder. Sometimes we'd like to reach out strictly because we know how much it would help to be held, and sometimes we are able to manage something similar to it.

I've heard it called a 'soul hug' and I'm not sure if I've ever thought of what to call it myself. It tends to manifest as a type of tingling, warm and emotional, which resonates throughout the body. It sometimes has the added effect of bringing a person to tears, which often happens when souls reach into one another. If you've ever had a very intense lovemaking session, you may recognize it as having merged souls to a small extent. People often feel this way after they have lost a close family member or friend, that feeling of someone near them and comforting them. I say this because it is far more likely that you will feel that way in their presence than feel someone watching you. In the latter instance, it tends to be your soul friend or other guide keeping an eye on you for various reasons.

If you suffer from some manner of anxiety about these kinds of things, say, you're home alone at night and you feel worried that someone is watching you, reach out with your mind and establish what type of person it is. If you feel nothing but that external, surface worry you should absolutely go investigate your house and check your windows. If you feel an emotional throb of sorts, question its familiarity and its intention. If it feels unfamiliar, you may just not recognize someone from your past or someone who is meant to be there. That's why intention is so important; those on our side cannot hide their intentions from you. If they mean you harm, and I remind you that is the very rarest of cases, you will know as soon as you ask it internally. If they are there to protect you it may be unsettling at first, but they will be able to convey that. That's part of the reason that projections of sympathy or love are prone to causing tears; they skip all doubt and pageantry and go straight to the heart.

I would say that none of us who are properly settled on this side ever say anything similar to "If I'd only been there, I would have…", though I've heard people on your plane say "If only so and so was here" more times than I could ever count. That's not how it works. Your life is your life and the presence of another would not have erased the pitfalls you were bound to face in this lifetime. If it had been avoided in one way, it would have come out in another. Say that you're facing a great deal of debt and feel that your departed spouse would have prevented this from happening – unfortunately, at the heart of the matter debt results from a lack of self-control on your part or someone else who is able to affect your finances. It may stem from pride or gluttony (and again this may not be your own) but if the presence of your spouse had prevented you from buying an extra designer bag, the pride might have manifested in excessive plastic surgery or the gluttony in over-eating. You cannot escape the things you need to work on and no one else can save you from those vices.

Once again, I do not judge. Over my many lifetimes I had a

multitude of failures, or 'as many as it took to improve myself' as I like to suggest. The underlined word here is 'myself', which is something that your loved ones know about you as well. I say with great certainty that they do not wish they could save you from your struggles, only that you didn't have to struggle and that they could be a support for you to overcome them on your own. They wish that they were present in a way that you could more easily recognize and feel, and if you want them there you have to see them without your earthly eyes. You know that – you do, if you allow yourself to go there. For many it's too difficult and painful; they feel the separation too acutely. Try to recognize that before they passed they were already separated from you by the space of a body, and if you let down your internal barriers for them they need not be separated from you at all but always present, always linked to you in your heart. Perhaps literally.

If you want to help yourself out, look at the problem on a grander scale. See it not as something in the present, in the single situation that you are facing, but a symptom of something abstract and timeless. People have faced pride, gluttony and all manner of shortcomings since the beginning of time; there is nothing to be ashamed of in having to battle that. Indeed, it may be the very reason you were born was to struggle against it and to overcome. If you feel that you need emotional strength to keep up the good fight, turn to us. We're always, always willing to give you that. And we will always wish that we didn't need to watch you struggle, that we could prevent the pain that accompanies learning a lesson, but we are also very proud of you for everything you survive and every time you grow stronger and wiser.

Reading the Design

SOMETIMES YOU MAY COME ACROSS unlikely scenarios either in your dreams, in your head or in the waking world. Perhaps you are seeing something you have already seen before as in déjà vu, or you know instinctively that something is happening elsewhere in the world while it is actually happening. Does this make you psychic?

Well, yes, in so far as everyone has the same abilities. Granted, the very youngest souls are not very good at this but most of the youngest souls haven't copped on to spirituality on a large scale. For the youngest souls, even when they find or are surrounded by religion, they tend to use it as a tool for their own ends instead of a moral compass or a framework from which to move about freely in the universe. What I want to say is that you too can do this, use this ability, at any time as long as you don't reject it subconsciously.

The reason these things don't happen to everyone and the reason they don't happen all the time is because you don't think they should. Have you ever guessed someone's name (or more likely something very close to it) on the first try? If it wasn't exactly right, it's because you knew the answer but didn't want to freak everyone out including yourself. I've been saying all along that collective consciousness is accessible to everyone, but only if you don't exclude yourself with your own sense of individuality.

In my opinion, it is best to think of oneself as a single embellishment in a huge blanket, there to create beauty and structure for everything around it. This blanket represents the entirety of the universe, particularly on your living level – it is the people on the Earth and everything within it as well as the energy fields that flow invisibly between them. Those energy fields are the bonds between things, the structural makeup. Why then is it so difficult to imagine that you have ways of knowing everything that goes on within this blanket you are a part of?

Mothers often say that they are able to tell when their children are sick or in danger even miles away. On the other hand, they may feel guilty if they don't – this phenomenon should demonstrate to you that people are infinitely connected no matter who they are. The point is that, between mothers and children, the bond is socially accepted just as it is accepted between twins. We say that when people have déjà vu or premonitions regarding people who are known to be deeply bonded (long-married couples are another example) that it's uncanny but not unusual. Why on earth would that bond only exist between certain types of people?

Now James, you might say, those people are close and not everyone is close to everyone else. I know that, but there's no reason for that either. People become close to one another because they allow people into their lives, yes? They let down their guards and their emotional and mental walls, they trust and they accept other people's energy into their space. If you want to read anything, whether it be other people's thoughts (I say this very cautiously) or the future, the past, the energy surrounding a place, if you want to speak to the dead – no matter what you do, it requires dropping your own barrier. Most people make the mistake of trying to think very hard to get inside whatever it is, to literally 'see inside' something. That's backwards! The true nature of whatever it is you want to know is there, you're just blocking it out with your sense of self and your sense of what is and isn't possible.

From now on I want you to try and view impossible things as accessing your own internal library, like a super computer connected to an infinite number of other computers. At the heart of this network is the source, and its energy flows out and in, out and in. (It feels very odd to speak of the energy of something that is in effect nothing but energy.) I want you to say, 'the answer is there' and look for it internally rather than externally. It may require meditation, but the better you get at lowering your walls the less difficulty you will have in accessing all of this extra information.

Finding the End of a Road

BY NOW YOU MAY HAVE guessed that the end of a road comes when you have no more options for growth in that particular scenario. This may mean a relationship, a job or even a location. Sometimes, as we have all experienced, it's time to leave.

So, when we've made up our minds that something needs to be done, we still struggle with the idea that it's up to us to make that leap. How do we know when the best time to do it is? How are we going to get by in the interim? The point is to listen to your heart. How very cheesy that sounds! But the truth is that a thing will work whether or not you expect it to if you approach it with right mindfulness. Now I'm starting to sound like a Buddhist, but his eightfold path had some very good ideas. Of those, I feel that going after things with the right frame of mind is the best one for success.

Let's imagine that you would like to lose weight or win the lottery. (Essentially, we are always looking to adjust levels and gain balance, no matter how much we would like odds tipped in our favour.) The chances of your success are always going to be relative to the why; why do you want this to happen, why should it happen in your life etc. The one thing you should never question is 'Why me and not someone else?' That very question is a falsehood. Your life path has nothing to do with the life paths of others, not as far as you are concerned. Never ever decide not to do something because you'd rather help someone else unless your actual goal is to help someone else. Don't stop at the finish line just to let another person win and don't give up what you know in your heart of hearts to be your purpose in life because it interferes with someone else.

Anyway, if you are meant to continue a journey with someone, those logistics will work themselves out and you need to have faith in that. If your partner is assigned to a job in Namibia and you are seeking to be a doctor, you may end up in Namibia with a lap full of medical books or that company may decide to start a branch in the town you choose to open your medical practice. If you are struggling, and by struggling I don't mean against each other but to take a step forward while still tied to one another, just unlace those ties and move forward. You'll discover soon enough that the ties you thought held you together were artificial and created in your brains, and that either the real ties that bind you will hold just as well as they always did or that you are suddenly burdened with wonderful freedom.

Have you ever ended a friendship and found it strange that you felt no guilt, only relief? That's because you removed those artificial ties. On the other hand, you may have divorced someone only to get remarried to them years later because your connection was one you could not control and in fact the artificial ties you placed on the relationship were interfering – they acted as a blindfold and little else. It's true that these relationships are rarely perfect, but if you've chosen to rekindle something or even reconcile with a relative or one of your children, either way you broke the false bonds from before and you'll view the connection in a different light.

So, trying to move on with things like money or food. The trick is to start off by finding the false connection first! It's a point to meditate on before you can make things work. Let's compare the problem of succeeding in this situation by comparing it to earlier humans and how they thought that frogs and other creatures could be spontaneously born from mud or straw. They saw creatures being born from somewhere in the ground and assumed that was how it was done. For people of today that seems ridiculous, but you'll one day look back on some of your current decisions and think they were ridiculous too. That's the very nature of enlightenment, only try not to judge yourself too harshly for it. So, what's your current scenario? I want money therefore the lottery is the answer? I don't want to give a lot of information here, mostly because I'm not allowed to go into great detail, but suffice it to say that the lottery is the straw or mud in this scenario. Please think about the end result and the beginning of the problem more deeply.

When people win vast amounts of money it isn't the money they are winning, but the effects of that money. Is there a lesson to be learned? Is there something to be put into motion by this event? What does money represent to them and more importantly to the world around them? When you ask to win the lottery, it is more likely that you are asking not to suffer or in many noble cases for your loved ones not to suffer. If you want to take a step forward with that in mind, by all means – seek the means to end that suffering in a positive, comfortable way. Be right minded. If your goal, your actual goal, is the abstract concept of money and its effects on the universe (as perhaps an experiment maybe?) then go ahead and ask for winning lottery numbers. In the end, people learn a difficult lesson or they don't change in the slightest. There is a reason for this.

Weight loss, too. How many times have you or others said, "It's time for me to walk away from this flab?" The scenario comes right back to a false bonding between you and the body you are locked in. Your image of the connection between your body being the way it is and yourself is incorrect, or else, coming to what you imagine to be the end of the road would actually work. Yo-yo diets, being unable to stick with diets, rebounds and all of those things are related to the real connection between you and your weight. It may be psychological, it may be medical or it may just be gluttonous, but whatever it is you haven't seen it yet. Every time in success stories regarding weight loss something finally stuck with these suddenly svelte people, but what I'm saying is you don't need to try every single method until something works. Figure out what the mud to your unattainable weight-loss frog is and take it from there. It may take some truth seeking, but once again if you have the right attitude – the right attitude for you, I mean, you will get there in no time. And always remember I love you just as you are.

Finally, I would like to discuss failed business ventures as the end of the road. Are you the type who can't stick with a job or who has been bankrupted several times? You're learning a lesson here and it hurts. It's awful, I very much sympathize – but you need right mindfulness. What you're doing at the moment is throwing something at the wall and seeing what sticks, which is the same struggle as people have with dieting and other pursuits of success. They aren't seeing the false connection that they need to break in order to get where they need to go. It seems to me you (or whoever in your life is going through this) have become convinced that something is a really fabulous idea to get rich quick or even just to get rich. The problem with that is the end goal. Being desperate because of the sting of poverty is understandable but you will continue to be desperate until you find what you need to contribute to the world. The easy part is that you already know it – it's that thing you can't seem to get away from no matter how you try. You might think it's lame or not lucrative enough, but somehow it keeps coming back to you. You're a doctor who can't give up surfing and only feels truly happy surrounded by waves or you're a plumber obsessed with programming. In those scenarios only, surfing will ever make you rich because it makes you rich inside. And no, I don't mean that in some abstract manner, I mean that only the thing you love like you were born to do it will ever get you business success in the entrepreneurial sense. Sometimes in the happiness sense as well. If you're wondering why you can't stay tied to some things and why you can't escape others, you may need to loosen some strings and accept the ones that you're bound to already. You can do it! Just be honest with yourself.

Snags in the Learning Process

OBVIOUSLY SOMETIMES THINGS WILL START off wonderfully and then fall apart or stagnate, and that's incredibly frustrating. There are a few reasons for this. The first one, the simplest one, is that the person you are talking to is a bit new to the soul friend business and they're impatient with how you can't seem to process what they're trying to tell you. That's not actually your fault, so long as you are making some sort of effort, so just tell them thank you and ask for someone else. They will go and they won't resent you for it, they'll more likely be disappointed in themselves than anything. Someone will take care of it and guide them for future endeavours on our side, so don't worry about it. They were just a bit overeager before they were ready.

Other times that person may be a sort of trainee soul friend to prepare you for the soul friend you are actually meant to have, because that soul friend may be on a higher level and too much to handle for a beginner. If so, congratulations as you are meant to impart some sort of wisdom via this soul friend. This is the difference between whether someone is meant to be there to help you through your darkest times or whether you're supposed to help others through their darkest times.

Translating from people who haven't been alive for a while can be trickier as their imagery is less tied to the physical plane and can come on an epic, confusing scale. Think babies crying in a temple of light or politicians arguing behind closed doors layered on top of skyscrapers crumbling. As I said, it's a bit much for someone who's new to the game, so sometimes there is a temporary soul friend sent in at first. If you feel like you've gone as far as you can with a soul friend you probably have. It's nothing to be guilty about and they won't feel like that either, I promise you that. Besides, once you've got things down pat you can call them back for a chat whenever you like – just meditate again from the very beginning and open yourself to a new person or new image and they should come when you're ready for them.

If you're not even getting to the first parts it's because of what I said earlier: you're not letting go or you're presupposing too much. If that's the problem, I recommend really just focusing on an image that repeats in a very neutral way. It doesn't have to be waves, it could be a continual image of wine swirling around a glass or dunes in a desert. It could be an endless sky (I recommend a blue one rather than other colours because it's default and it carries pure and happy connotations) or as one of my compatriots suggests, a stalk of bamboo. Picture how green and smooth it is, how cold it is beneath your fingers, how the bumps between each section feel – he recommends it highly if you're in pain and looking to take your mind off of things.

The final technique I'd like to mention is the frosted glass window technique, which is good again if you're feeling anxious or trying to push yourself too hard. Start with picturing a window outside of a home in all of the detail that you can muster, but it's covered in frost from the cold or else it has been designed that way. There is a warm light beyond that window, a happy scene of some sort, but you can't see it. Try and peer in through the window and make out the details in whatever way you can. If it's from the cold, you can even try heating it with your breath or wiping it with your hands, but don't think that your goal is anything beyond 'see what is on the other side of this window'. Happy meditating!

The Journey from Here

You will hear from a great variety of sources that the next millennium will be full of change. (Author's note: I said millennium was too large a scope, but James insisted.) The point is that we are on the beginning of a wave that is destined to rise, crest and fall, but in falling bring with it a new era. It will wash away the dirt of the past and make learning take on a whole new meaning.

Until now we have been burdened by the fear and hatred that makes ascension so difficult, but right now we may view the ship of humanity as breaking free from the tethers that hold it to the shore. I mean this in a great many ways, and for those of you who are thinking of space I mean this too. When we were young, at the dawn of humanity, we were preoccupied with the progress of tiny things like learning how to use fire and new kinds of weaponry, but as we move forward we cannot remain on the same level. The things that have always stayed with us, those eternal truths that speak of love and wonderment, will always be with us, but we cannot grow – even the same souls cannot grow – from the learning of souls previous. Essentially saying, history repeating is not progress and so history itself has to be redefined.

One way of doing this is through the exploration of time as a concept – the idea of time as it is incredibly flawed, unfortunately, and only functions as an arbitrary construct that does more harm than good. If you were not stressed by the constraints of time or burdened by the idea that things come and are taken away rather than merely existing one on top of another, you would certainly not experience grief and loss in the same manner. As I say, time itself needs to be rethought in order to make progress. That is the first step.

The second step is that we need to view the world as one and in a different light. Boundaries are also arbitrary constructs decided by small people, small minds, and they need to be done away with before we can move on. It goes back to what I have been trying to explain this entire book – that you are the universe, and that in looking at things as differences you are doing yourself a disservice. Anyone who believes that they cannot be both black and white, red and brown, a child of the world and all of the things in it, has not reached the place they need to in order to ride this wave. As to whether or not people will be able to do so – of course they will. The thing is that those who cannot enter the new path will be dashed by the wayside (an awful image, I know) and be reborn again and again until they are able to fit into this new scheme. Things that are not meant to take root never will, and that is a fact.

I don't want you to think that I am being cruel and that I am prophesying some sort of massive culling. That is not the case. What I am saying is that phrase that goes 'when I was a child, I thought like a child' and now that we would be adults, we have to change. It would be accurate to say that the world up until this current time has been in teenagerhood, I think. The strife is very similar to the rebellious phase and it occurs to people that in order to move forward that sort of behaviour is not acceptable. Any soul that is reborn and tries to live in a manner befitting a child or a teenager will not thrive and will return to our realm to think about it before trying once again. I don't expect the re-attempt rate to take more than one lifetime. The thing is that as the human mind grows, the previous challenges are no longer satisfactory in training new thought processes. Change, as it were, is inevitable.

Regarding that second step I mentioned, I fear that some people think that they will lose their culture if they do not honour the differences between them and those of other countries or backgrounds, but even now people come in a vast many version that somehow live harmoniously together. Just think; if it has been conceived of, it is part of the human conscious collective. There is no way that you will ever lose the things that make you special, certainly not on this earth, just as 'they' will never lose theirs. And you are one, you are them and they you, so you should respect those points. Boundaries are a foundation of loss just as time is the greatest of those boundaries.

How you can help in ushering in this new era is by devoting your thoughts to the great collective consciousness, that being the single mind shared by the earth, but in particular by humanity. As I say, it's a bit hard to think of oneself as the same as and yet one tiny piece of the universe. Let's start with raising our minds to the singular idea of existence and nothing more than that: just think to yourself, I am a part of this. We is me, me is we. Picture yourself breaking down the barriers of time. Picture lighthouses standing where parking lots are now, and castles in the place of skyscrapers. This is all from the same Source and that Source is eternal, and so you are connected with not only every living thing right now but every thing that has ever lived or been thought up, and all of the power within that is within you just as you contribute to that power with every idea you have and with every idea that makes you up. Thinking that way and treating your days in that manner will not only benefit you immensely but also benefit the whole of mankind. It sounds outrageous, but there it is.

Biography

JESSICA CRICHTON WAS BORN IN Edinburgh, Scotland in 1984. She grew up in Ontario, Canada and currently resides in Tokyo, Japan with her husband. She received her degree, a double major in English and Japanese, from McMasters University, Ontario
   Jessica is a writer, translator, interpreter and artist. She currently enjoys writing copy and original stories and content as well as translating. She has been talking to James since she was a child, living with his wisdom and sharing it with others. You can follow more of James' writings on:

YOUARENEVERLOST.BLOGSPOT.COM